TRANSGRESSIVE

of related interest

To My Trans Sisters
Edited by Charlie Craggs
ISBN 978 1 78592 343 2
eISBN 978 1 78450 668 1

How to Understand Your Gender
A Practical Guide for Exploring Who You Are
Alex Iantaffi and Meg-John Barker
Foreword by S. Bear Bergman
ISBN 978 1 78592 746 1
eISBN 978 1 78450 517 2

First Year Out
A Transition Story
Sabrina Symington
ISBN 978 1 78592 258 9
eISBN 978 0 85701 303 3

Queer Sex
A Trans and Non-Binary Guide to Intimacy,
Pleasure and Relationships
Juno Roche
ISBN 978 1 78592 406 4
eISBN 978 1 78450 770 1

Everything You Ever Wanted to Know
about Trans (But Were Afraid to Ask)
Brynn Tannehill
ISBN 978 1 78592 826 0
eISBN 978 1 78450 956 9

TRANS-GRESSIVE

A TRANS WOMAN ON GENDER, FEMINISM, AND POLITICS

Rachel Anne Williams

Jessica Kingsley *Publishers*
London and Philadelphia

First published in 2019
by Jessica Kingsley Publishers
73 Collier Street
London N1 9BE, UK
and
400 Market Street, Suite 400
Philadelphia, PA 19106, USA

www.jkp.com

Library of Congress Cataloging in Publication Data
A CIP catalog record for this book is available from the Library of Congress

British Library Cataloguing in Publication Data
A CIP catalogue record for this book is available from the British Library

ISBN 978 1 78592 647 1
eISBN 978 1 78592 648 8

Printed and bound in the United States

To all the trans feminists
who have gone before me
and those who never made it.

CONTENTS

Metaphysics and Epistemology — 171

Autobiographical Notes — 211

PREFACE

This book has its origins in a blog I started three years ago when I first came out to myself.[1] Prior to that, I had been blogging for years, mostly about philosophy and psychology but also whatever I happened to be fascinated by, and I had always wanted to collect my best online writing and put it in a book. In grad school, the book project got away from me, put on a back burner while I was in the throes of figuring out this thing we call "gender" and trying to write a dissertation. I continued to write for my blog but the topics shifted from psychology and consciousness to feminism, gender studies, trans theory, and so on. These days, as I contemplate the idea of being "post-transition," I find my mind being drawn back into the hodgepodge of interests that has always defined my research style.

For a long time, writing was something akin to a hobby for me. It was not until I met my now recent ex-girlfriend that I was able to see my writing through someone else's eyes and gain some confidence in my ability. And thus, this collection was born.

My passion for philosophy goes back to an honors intro-ductory course I took in college at the University of Central Florida, where I fell in love with the crazy concepts, questions, and thought experiments, the employment of the careful distinction, the precision in language, and exploration of mind-bending ideas and reflections of utter moral seriousness. I was drawn to the philosophy of religion, existentialism, and phenomenology. I was also interested in consciousness, philosophy of mind, cognitive science, and the intersection therein. What is the nature of the mind? And how does it fit into the physical world? These questions occupied me for almost a decade with their fractal complexity.

My undergraduate degree was a "build-your-own" degree called Interdisciplinary Studies. You had to choose two main fields of study and also a minor. My fields were philosophy and the social sciences, with a minor in cognitive science. Basically, it was the quickest route to graduation that allowed me to take the most classes I was interested in and minimize the number of classes I had to take that I was not interested in. If it was not already immediately obvious from my degree choices, I smoked a *ton* of pot in college.

After my first degree, I left Orlando for Baton Rouge, where I spent two years getting my Master's in philosophy while drinking Purple Haze on draft from local pizza joints and eating Cajun food. There was a fucking *tiger* kept in what seemed like a small cage on campus. The whole school was constantly hyped about football, and the whole campus revolved around the games—I only attended one and came away with distinct religious/ culty vibes.

Louisiana State University (LSU) was considered a "continental" philosophy program and I wrote my Master's thesis on some thorny ontological problems in Heidegger's *Being and Time.* LSU was a time of intellectual productivity and led to my only single-author, peer-reviewed publication, a manifesto of sorts defending an obscure Princeton psychologist Julian Jaynes and his theory of consciousness.

After Baton Rouge, I was fortunate enough to get into my dream PhD (doctoral) program at Washington University in St. Louis—the philosophy-neuroscience-psychology program. It was essentially a normal six-year philosophy PhD program but we had to take tons of classes in the world-famous neuroscience and psychology departments. I spent a lot of time learning about brain imaging. I took classes with the people who essentially invented functional magnetic resonance imaging (fMRI), the technique famous for giving birth to phrases like "The visual area of the brain lit up like a Christmas tree."

I was in grad school when I decided to transition. My wife had left me for someone she fell for when we had an open marriage— he was a rich and successful anesthesiologist and I was a lowly grad student years away from making any real money. I had recently gotten out of the psychiatric ward (see essay 37, "That's so crazy!"), a complete fucking mess, and I had fallen in her eyes from the strong husband she had been in love with to a weak, helpless, sorry excuse of a man with a penchant for women's clothing. The marriage was doomed.

When she announced the end of our marriage, the first thoughts that crossed my mind involved a sudden realization that I was free to explore my gender, something that I had been strongly but indirectly discouraged from doing throughout the entirety of our marriage. It was exhilarating knowing that now, finally, nothing was stopping me from transitioning, or at the very least taking my gender exploration further than before.

It was fucking terrifying. I remember being on Google and looking up facts and statistics about being a trans woman and the numbers scared me: what was I in for? Was it really worth it? If my brief internet research was to be trusted, it seemed as if my life as a trans woman would involve nothing but destitution, discrimination, and sex work. Even my mother expressed concerns I'd be lonely forever because, obviously, who would love a fucked-up tranny?

As it turns out, I could never have predicted how my transition would unfold, nor could I fully appreciate at the time the full extent of my inner vision for how I want my life to go— which is starting to become much clearer three years on. But I can say now, with absolute certainty, it was worth it. And far from destitution and loneliness, transition has led me to explore the depths of love and relationships like never before with poly, kinky, queer and trans folk. I have found my community.

Before I transitioned, I had been working on a dissertation proposal about detecting consciousness in the vegetative state using fMRI technology. But having grown frustrated with the whole field of consciousness studies, and going through the throes of transition, I found my academic research interests shifting into feminism, gender studies, and, more specifically, the scholarly issues surrounding the topic of being trans ("trans studies").

I ended up focusing my new dissertation topic on the ethical issues involving transgender healthcare, concentrating specifically on gatekeeping and the alternative informed consent model. And so began my foray into the world of trans feminism, gender politics, legal studies, LGBT+ (lesbian, gay, bisexual and transgender/transsexual plus) history, trans healthcare, psychology, the science of gender difference, and many other topics that intersect with trans studies. I dropped out of my PhD program in my last year, half-way through my dissertation. This was a decision based on both my disillusionment with academia in general and the subtle value changes that occurred as a result of gender transition, itself a polite term for a momentous shift in my entire perspective on reality, my place in society, and my daily phenomenological reality.

But throughout this time, I continued to do public philosophy on my blog. At first, writing about trans issues was difficult because I was overwhelmed with how much I had to learn. I still feel overwhelmed, but I have at least developed a voice. I used my blog as a kind of phenomenological journal to work through my experiences during transition as well as to explore some of the theoretical issues in trans politics that I found interesting. Initially, a lot of my thinking was a way of working through the body of trans literature that has come before me. Eventually, however, I gained enough confidence for my work to *be* trans feminism rather than be *about* trans feminism (though I reserve the right, of course, to analyze and comment on existing literature).

After almost three years of blogging on trans issues from the perspective of an academically trained philosopher, I decided to select the best essays I had written, revise and expand them, and turn them into the book you are now reading. I also threw in five new essays written for this collection.[2] In total there are 40 essays. They are roughly organized by theme but they do not need to be read in any particular order. My ideal is for the reader to simply scroll through the table of contents until they find a title that sounds interesting—rinse and repeat.

The first section, "Transfeminine Blues," is about some of the struggles that trans feminine people face in a world set out to morally mandate us out of existence, to beat us down and kill us. The section also discusses some of my personal experiences with dysphoria, being read as ambiguous, issues with "passing," and my growth as a trans woman. The second section, "Feminist Musings," is about the intersection between trans life and feminism as a field of study. In this section, I write about sapiosexualism, cat-calling, the gender wars, dysphoria, and the history of trans feminism. In the third section, "Life in Transition," I talk about my experiences transitioning from male-to-female and some of the struggles I faced (and continue to face) throughout this process. In the fourth section, "Gender and Politics," I discuss some of the political debates within feminism concerning whether dysphoria is necessary for being trans, so-called "gender critical feminism," the politics of passing, and autogynephilia. In the fifth section, "Metaphysics and Epistemology," I talk about the philosophical questions that being trans raises such as: what is gender identity? How do we know we are trans? Can you be trans without transitioning? How is sex different from gender? Is it possible to change one's sex? Is gender nihilism a coherent philosophical position? In the final section, "Autobiographical Notes," I write about some of my personal experiences involving male privilege, dating lesbians as a trans woman, ableism and mental illness, how to make personal finance queer, and my own relationship to fetishism. The final section includes further resources for the reader's own pursuit of gender studies and feminism.

All the essays are relatively short. They are (I hope) written in plain English but tackle some pretty complex topics. My goal was not to flesh out ideas in mind-numbing detail—my preferred style of argumentation is purely suggestive. I want merely to stimulate the imagination, to explore new ideas and let the reader fill in the details on their own. Although I was trained in analytic (and continental) style philosophy, I prefer writing in the easy style of classic American prose—"Clear and Simple as the Truth"[3]— often shooting for that sweet spot of around 1000 words. Have five or ten minutes to spare? Read one of the essays and let it turn over in your mind. Or binge-read ten essays in a row if you're a fast reader (fair warning: the essays are not necessarily "easy" to read on an emotional level—I know at least they were not easy to write).

There is no right way to read this book. And feel free to disagree with me (shoot me an email or Tweet or comment on my blog) about anything I say. I typically aim to maintain a state of agnosticism about almost everything relating to philosophy, gender, feminism, or even my own identity. Part of this is simply a defense mechanism against my own internalized shit. But part of it is a deep skepticism that runs through my personality as well as an unwillingness to take a firm stance on something that is hard to operationalize, and thus settle in a public, consensus-oriented manner.

One of the things I have learned since I started writing on trans/queer topics is that the best policy is to always stay in my lane. And by that I really do mean: *my* lane. I should only be writing about *my* trans experience and not extrapolate that to other trans people because everyone is different, has a different set of life experiences, assumptions, values, beliefs, and so on, and it would be pure hubris to think that I could somehow act as a voice to represent all trans people. Nobody can do that. And if it comes off that way in anything I write below, I apologize ahead of time—I am still learning to stay in my lane.

Another thing I have learned from writing for an LGBT+ audience is that queer/trans folks *really* care about language and the devil is in the details. I always put a lot of thought into the particular words I use but I recognize that not everyone is going to be happy with certain linguistic choices made in these essays. For example, my usage of the t-slur might make some uncomfortable. But in the end, I hope if I can convey anything to my audience it's that I care deeply about this community—this entire project started as a labor of love. While I would love to make a living from writing on these issues, if I never made a dollar I would still be blogging, writing, listening, and sharing with this wonderful community.

My absolute favorite part of blogging over all these years has been getting the random email from someone half-way across the world who was positively impacted by my writing. That fucking means everything to me—I am getting slightly emotional just thinking about it. What a privilege. I realize I have a tremendous responsibility with this platform. And there is a temptation, in you, the reader, to bestow my voice with a special significance because of that platform.

But I encourage skepticism of everything I say in this volume. I am fallible. I am biased. I am ignorant of many things. I am, above all, human, "all too human" as Nietzsche said. While it's true I have read a lot of fancy books in my years of graduate training that does not necessarily give me the wisdom to properly interpret that knowledge and translate it into feminist thought. If I achieve anything close to that, it is a proper achievement, not to be assumed the default state of my writing.

Therefore, dear reader, I am giving you a job. You have responsibility as a reader. I want you read my work critically. Critical reading is different from easy reading. Easy reading is letting the information flow through your mind. Critical reading is trying to find all the holes in the argument.

But I have an even greater job for you. I want you to engage in both critical reading *and* constructive reading. Constructive reading is reading with an eye for improvement: how can this idea be made better? How can we work together to create a better vocabulary, a better conceptual toolkit to understand the world? But also: what am I missing? Whose voice have I left out? Am I going outside my lane? Show me. But please do it gently. In grad school, we learned a technique called the "shit sandwich." You start with a compliment, then the criticism, then another compliment. So please, make me a shit sandwich.

R.A.W.
St. Louis, 2018

TRANS FEMININE BLUES

1

TRANS PORN, TRANS WOMEN, AND THE FETISHIZATION OF "T-GURLS"

Porn featuring trans women, also known as "tranny porn," has always been popular among straight men and continues to be widely popular. Moreover, if you want to be a trans porn star, you better not cut your dick off because the fetishization of women with penises is at the very heart of why trans porn is so popular.

But why?

Why are men so obsessed with my penis? I have been on Tinder for years since starting transition and the average length of time for any man to go from introduction to "Have you had 'the surgery'?" is five minutes. And it's not just men—there are female chasers out there as well. Cis people are desperate to know if I've cut it off already or when I am going to "fully transition" (I call that a cis-ism because it's so predictable).[1] And lest we fool ourselves, there are also trans people who fetishize other trans people. How exactly we define "fetishization" is tricky—we can return to that later—but needless to say there are degrees, and the boundaries between "extreme preference," "problematic fetish," "permissible fetish," and everything in-between are quite fuzzy.

Regardless, how could it be that many straight men would not date, love, or marry a trans woman but will jerk off to her on the internet? If you want to see the fetishization of trans women happen in real time just go to Craigslist's "m4t" personals section and read and weep.[2]

Straight men will fuck us, but not love us.

All they care about is that we are "passable," that we are "smooth and femme." Chasers don't care that we are strong, determined women with complex lives and unique insights into the world—they just want to suck our dicks without feeling too gay.

They don't really see us as females, they see us as a third sex, an Other. We are never simply women, or even trans women, but rather trannies, t-girls, gurls, t-gurls, transsexuals, TS, TS gurls, shemales, ladyboys, he/shes, chicks with dicks, and so on, and so on. Even within the binary, we are either unnatural women or strange boys, but never exemplars of our proclaimed genders.

What's the one glaring difference between cis porn and trans porn? The genitals are different. But why do straight men consume so much porn featuring women with not-commonly-seen genitals? I hypothesize that two primary factors are at play: novelty and taboo.

For straight men used to having sex with cis women and watching porn of cis women, trans women represent something they see as "exotic," possibly even "alien," yet at the same time very familiar; after all, these women have penises and the men have penises so there is thus a shared bond that creates the fantasy of an erotic connection. For straight cis men, the vagina is a mystery. A penis, however, is straightforward—there are no inner chambers, or hidden mysteries.[3]

Trans women make up roughly 1 percent of the population. Many Americans don't personally know any trans people. Perhaps they have seen some of the not-so-great representations in the media: Jerry Springer, *Ace Ventura*, *SVU*, Buffalo Bill, *Dallas Buyers Club*, Frank N. Furter, *The Crying Game*, and so on. Perhaps they have heard of Caitlyn Jenner or maybe saw what could have been a trans woman at the mall once.

But you bet they've seen trans porn. It's all over the internet.

Our rarity makes us anomalies to the cis world, strange creatures who are "othered" so strongly that we become a separate metaphysical category: the *t-gurl*.

When you combine the novelty factor with the social stigma against trans bodies it creates a taboo whereby trans porn becomes "dirty," "naughty," or otherwise scandalous. This is why straight male celebrities who get "caught" dating trans women often end up in media scandals and their manhood is called into question. As Julia Serano writes in *Whipping Girl*, "Trans women are hypersexualized in our culture because we are viewed as enabling our own sexual objectification (by virtue of the fact that we physically transition from male to female)."[4]

This why so many straight men might hook up with trans women but do not bring them to Thanksgiving dinner. The taboo nature of trans people, and especially trans women, fuels our fetishization. When straight men consume too much cis porn they become bored and may be drawn to the novelty and stigma of trans porn. This accounts for its long-term, overwhelming popularity among straight cis men while at the same time it is not something most men would openly admit to their male friends.

Why does this matter? Let me give you a scenario drawn from real life. A straight cis male is horny, watching trans porn.

He gets so horny that he wants to find a trans girl to fulfill his fantasy. He goes on Craigslist and finds someone.[5] He has sex with her, cums, and then has a sudden feeling of disgust, his sense of being a straight man now threatened because he possibly got off on her having a dick, or was disgusted by the idea that he "just fucked a dude." He gets enraged and defensive, "panics," and then assaults and/or murders the trans woman for having the audacity to be herself.

I am not making up this scenario at all. It is taken from real life, often involving trans women of color, sex workers, the marginalized, and many trans and non-binary people, especially those on the trans feminine spectrum. I have talked with many trans women about this and their testimony usually shares a similar motif. My own casual sexual experiences with men were never without that hypothetical scenario somewhere in the back of my mind.

Sadly, this so-called "panic defense" is admissible in court as an excuse for murder in most states. This is why the fetishization of trans women is so dangerous. Too many men want to fuck us (or be fucked by us) yet are so poisoned by transphobia that they reflexively feel the need to defend their masculinity after sleeping with us. Or maybe they will skip the sex and just kill us for trying to "trick" them if we don't explicitly out ourselves.

It happens. All the time. All across the world. So next time you internally "other" a trans woman, remember, your attitude of fetishization and objectification of her body is indirectly fueling violence against trans bodies. Your fetish is not innocent.

But don't get me wrong, there is nothing wrong with being attracted to trans bodies. I get it, trust me: trans people are beautiful and our bodies are special and wonderful as well. The problem is not finding trans women attractive, or even being super turned on by the uniqueness of our bodies, it's the automatic mental operation of putting us into the metaphysical category of an Other, an automatic third sex option ticked off. It's why it's so common for straight men to only call us "gurls" because they want to highlight how we are so different from cis girls. We become a whole other creature: a tranny.

There is nothing wrong with third gender, or thinking that you are third gender or otherwise outside the binary. I often think of myself as third gender. It's what I feel most comfortable with. But I would never say that all other trans people are third gender, because many are firmly within the gender binary and I respect that. It's the way in which we are thrown into the third sex/gender category without our explicit consent. It's the way our bodies are seen as exotic and otherworldly, like a living, breathing sex doll with "unique features." This widespread attitude is dangerous and fuels much of the transphobic violence against trans women.

If we are going to put an end to transphobic violence and the dangerous fetishization of trans bodies, we need to, as a society, become more accepting of trans people, especially trans women, as normal members of society, not deviants or perverts or otherwise sub-classes of normal people. We need to end the Jerry Springer-esque "freak show" phenomenon that fuels the stigma against us.

2

TRANS WOMEN AND MALE PRIVILEGE

There has been a lot of ink spilled lately about trans women and male privilege. People are concerned with the question: "Do trans women as a whole have male privilege and if so what kind and how much?"

Some trans women respond to this question by arguing, "The idea of male privilege/male socialization doesn't match my experience," and then going on to detail how their lives were not filled with anything resembling typical straight, cis, male privilege and how in fact they were brutalized for being feminine as "boys" and in fact did not internalize society's messages about male socialization the same way "normal" boys did.

But then in response to *those* articles, some trans women are writing articles saying, "I *did* have male privilege but I gave it up or am in the process of giving it up. Oh and by the way I'm still a woman."

Some of these articles also make the general claim that male privilege was afforded to *all* trans women in virtue of being coded as male pre-transition regardless of how it was internalized.

In other words, if you are perceived by society as male then you have male privilege in virtue of that coding. This is a highly contentious claim. Other trans women deny this reflects their own experience growing up and they share their stories of being brutalized and lacking privilege in virtue of their femininity—being perceived as a "sissy" boy afforded them little privilege.

This debate just goes around in a circle, with universal claims being negated by individual claims and individual claims being taken as proof of some universal claim. This is not a very productive debate.

Unfortunately, I suspect that the human brain is wired to prefer simplistic models of the universe and narratives about *all* trans women are easier to propagate than narratives that focus on our individuality and diversity—after all, keeping track of all that concrete particularity is more complicated than simply shoving seven billion people into one of two boxes. In my opinion, trans women and indeed all trans folk (and probably everyone else on the planet too) are best understood on a case-by-case basis when it comes to the complexities of gender.

Science is about averages, but in reality nobody is really average. We are all highly complex beings with unique life histories. It's naive to expect a clean and tidy theory about *all* trans women simply because they have in common a doctor looking in at their external genitalia on birth and declaring "boy." That's it. That's what these women have in common.

But rather than using *that* as the entire theoretical apparatus to explain why a trans woman did this or that, or appealing to some "male essence" shared by all trans women, we should instead look to a more complex story involving our genetic-epigenetic-social-learning history.

Thus, the structure of the dialectic works like this: we have a general claim about *all* trans women being refuted by individual claims about *some* trans women. But the trans women who did not experience themselves as having male privilege often make the same mistake of thinking their experience is universal. That's what's so wrong with this whole discussion. There are no universals. There are no generalizations to be made in terms of *all* trans women—every trans woman has a different experience of living pre-transition and post-transition with regard to privilege.

Furthermore, people like to frame the discussion in terms of the pointless question of whether trans women's experiences are identical to cis women's experiences. But who cares? It doesn't matter if they are *identical*—they need only be similar. Our experiences don't need to perfectly match the cis experience to be representative of womanhood because to think otherwise is to buy into the cis-sexist belief that the cis experience is the "default" and the trans experience is a pale imitation. But, in reality, the trans experience is equally valid, it's just exceedingly rare and happens to take a more convoluted pathway.

My own experience pre-transition featured a good deal of male privilege. I've retained some vestiges of that male privilege such as having grown up internalizing the stereotype that my gender was inherently more "rational." I still have the privilege of not worrying about getting pregnant (though for other trans women this is not a privilege at all but a curse, further underscoring the contextual nature of privilege).

But much of the male privilege I once had is gone. I now fear walking down the street at night whereas before I never did (at least not the for same reasons now). I now fear cat-calling and being discovered for being a "trap"—before it was not even on my mind. I've lost the privilege of not worrying about my drink being drugged at a bar. I've lost the privilege of being taken seriously as a rational thinker free of emotional bias—now I am just a crazy "Tranny SJW (social justice warrior)" gone wild. The list goes on.

Privilege is rarely monolithic or one-dimensional. My privilege as an educated white person and the vestigial remains of my male privilege are balanced against my loss of privilege as a woman and especially as a trans woman. Throw in my own struggles with dysphoria and the minority stress of being visibly trans and it doesn't seem all that privileged, though, of course, I reserve the right to take advantage of my trans status if the opportunity presents itself—girl's gotta feed herself.

But my experience says nothing about the experiences of other trans women, who likely experienced their gender quite differently from the way I did as a child and as I do now. I was never really made fun of for being feminine—my feminine behaviors were done in secret behind closed doors and so they weren't a target for explicit harassment. I was able to regiment my personality into a public boyish self and a private feminine self. But this process of privatizing my desires led to an intense cycle of shame and guilt, occasionally purging my feminine things only to later acquire them anew. It was a private little heaven inside a larger hell.

It's a myth that gender identity is formed for life within the first five years of life. While that might be true for many people, it is not a universal truth as my own life is a clear counter-example (and internet research tells me I'm not alone). My gender identity has evolved significantly since I was 5 years old and I know I am not alone, although I have the feeling that many trans people have a bias towards interpreting their memories as having an earlier regimented identity because that narrative is seen as "more valid" than the ones where gender identity evolution occurs later in life. There is intense pressure to make our stories palatable to cis people because our lives are already under so much scrutiny.

Not all young trans girls are able to hide their natural femininity and they are brutalized for it. If someone went through that experience and they are telling you they did not have male privilege, then I believe it's epistemically best practice to heed what they are saying and take their narrative seriously. Likewise, if a trans woman says she used to have male privilege but has since given most of it up, we need to listen to that narrative as well.

And even if you disagree with this self-assessment, ask yourself why you are so invested in finding the "truth" in this instance. What's so important about drilling down to the "reality" of whether trans women "truly" have male privilege? I have always been attracted to the pragmatic tradition in philosophy, which connects the concept of "truth" more closely to what works for us (where the idea of what "works" does imply an objective sense of running up against reality). And furthermore, we might ask ourselves: what works for trans people? Listening to our stories at face value? Or applying a theoretical notion of privilege that doesn't fit with lived experience? At the end of the day, we have to ask ourselves: what's the point of even developing a theory of gender?

Furthermore, cis people seem to be more convinced that if a trait is displayed earlier in life it is "more natural" and thus a product of someone's core essence. But that's the wrong assumption to be making. Innate or not, natural or not, what we should care about is if a behavior, trait, or personality is authentic and representative of someone's deepest vision for how they want their life to go, regardless of the "origins" of that vision.

If someone's trans identity originated in their 40s, that does not make their trans identity less authentic than someone whose trans identity originated in childhood. If someone starts painting in their 40s, does that make them "less" of a painter than someone who has been painting since infancy? A painter is someone who paints. A trans person is someone with a gender identity different from their assigned gender. It's not "gender identity different from assigned gender but also having emerged by 5 years old." It just has to be different. But the causal origins of the identity itself in terms of when it originated in the lifeline are not relevant for the authenticity of the identity.

My trans identity only surfaced in my late 20s. It would be *so* easy and no one could prove me wrong if I began saying things like: "I felt off during puberty but I only learned the words to articulate my feelings years later." In a sense that would be perfectly true. I did have gender issues at a young age. But I think I would be deluding myself if I claimed I had any awareness of ever wanting to transition at that age. Just as gender identity doesn't have to be cemented in childhood, neither does dysphoria have to originate in childhood. Dysphoria can surface at any point in a trans person's life. I didn't start feeling real, high-level, intense dysphoria until my late 20s. The longer we hold on to the traditional narrative that all trans people somehow "knew" when they were children, the longer we will be unable to see the true diversity of the trans community.

The problem comes when we try to generate a one-size-fits-all theoretical framework for thinking about *all* trans women as sharing some kind of universal essence. That's a pipedream. There is no universal narrative. The human mind strives to "connect the dots" and create some kind of overarching generalization that is true of all trans women. But we need to resist that and instead focus on studying individual differences. As Max Wolf Valerio writes in *The Testosterone Files*, "Transsexual identities must be defined and expressed on our own terms. Our voices are unique and, until recently, unheard and incompletely imagined."[6]

3

TRANNIES, TRAPS, AND THE THIRD GENDER

Caitlyn Jenner's reality TV show *I Am Cait* featured a debate between two well-known trans writers, Kate Bornstein and Jenny Boylan. Kate Bornstein is well known for being a theatrical, queer, radical activist type and Jenny Boylan is an English professor and more literary in her approach to gender issues.

That contrast set up a debate about the word "tranny." Bornstein famously identifies as a "tranny" whereas Boylan argues that the word is a slur and trying to reappropriate the word is bad for trans people because it places us into a fetishized, objectified "third gender." Bornstein retorts that it's her right to reappropriate "tranny" for herself just like some gay people have reappropriated "queer," a powerful word that was once used entirely as a weapon of violence against gender and sexual minorities but has now become a term lovingly adopted by many in the LGBT+ community. As she famously wrote in *Gender Outlaw,* "I know I am not a man—about that much I'm very clear, and I've come to the conclusion I'm probably not a woman either, at least not according to a lot of people's rules on this sort of thing."[7]

There is similar debate happening in online circles about whether the word "trap" is a slur and if it's possible for trans girls to reappropriate this term for themselves. A "trap" is basically a trans girl or crossdresser who "tricks" or "traps" a straight male into getting aroused by them and then suddenly reveals their trans status. "Trap" has now just come to be a colloquial internet term for any trans feminine person, often used in forums populated by men that share trans porn. The more "passable" the trans girl, the better the "trap."

It's easy to see why the whole culture surrounding traps is harmful to trans women. First, it conflates trans women with crossdressers, femboys, sissies, and so on. Second, it perpetuates the plainly false idea that trans women only transition in order to seduce or trick men. Third, and this is the one I want to discuss in more detail, "trap" is a kind of third-gendering whereby trans girls are put into the category of something other than male/female— they are a Third thing, a t-gurl, tranny, trap, shemale, he/she, ladyboy. This automatic third-gendering is harmful because it invalidates the womanhood of trans women by assuming our identity is inherently "not normal," that we cannot just be normal women, with normal proclivities and a normal demeanor.

However, there is nothing wrong with identifying as a third gender if that's what you are comfortable with. The automatic imposition of that category is dangerous but there is nothing inherently wrong with identifying outside the gender binary, especially given that gender binary itself is a product of colonial power.

Personally, I have taken solace in my identity as third gender, a *trans woman* (not a "woman"), because it is useful to me as a defense mechanism against TERFs[8] and their demand for me to define "womanhood" apart from stereotypes of femininity, socialization, and normal cis female anatomy. They say I have no right to claim "womanhood." And so I don't. I am not a woman. I am a tranny. A trans woman. A trans person. A non-binary trans femme. Whatever. I don't even know what I am. I don't spend a lot of time agonizing over finding the perfect label. For some folks, these things are important but not so much for me.

But it's funny. Despite my reluctance to identify as a woman I run into so many friendly cis female allies who welcome me enthusiastically into womanhood and assume automatically that I want to be 100 percent *lady*. And yes, of course, obviously I want to be in woman-only spaces. But my right to be there should not necessarily be based on whether I identify to the full extent as a binary woman with no internal psychological reservations about binaryism. I believe non-binary trans femmes also have a place in spaces that focus on excluding men even if they are more comfortable with a gender outside the usual two options.

For me personally, I tend to use the word "tranny" as something I feel comfortable using around my trans partner and/or trans people I'm close to (and some cis folks) but it would annoy me if a cis person ever tried to use the word, even in good jest. It's for *us* to play with. It's a venting mechanism and coping strategy that allows me to use self-deprecation to manage internalized transphobia.

For me, "tranny" is a way of taking the objectification and dehumanization of my identity and sublimating it into a term of endearment that I use to vent about how I'm perceived in society. Thus, Bornstein's *identification* with "tranny" is something that deeply resonates with me. It goes beyond mere venting—it bores down into my internal feelings of having an abominable gender.

I don't know how much of that identification is due to a lifetime of growing up with the cultural background knowledge of how trans people are treated—Jerry Springer curiosities who have the power to make men throw up (according to the infamous scene in *Ace Ventura*)—or how much of my internal identification with "tranny" comes from a genuine ownership of being an Other. I have always given little fucks about what society thinks and I very much feel comfortable around non-conformists.

I want to emphasize at this point that my intuitive leanings towards the Bornstein view of things is totally idiosyncratic—I recognize that other trans people are going to have different feelings about this issue and readily sympathize with the Boylan position. Many trans folks do *not* identify as freaks or traps or trannies or whatever—they identify firmly as being simple, normal, boring men and women, normal members of their gender class who just have a unique (and private) medical history involving congenital hormone abnormalities, and so on.

I think this sort of view is totally valid. There's nothing wrong with identifying as just a "man" or "woman." So often trans people hear, especially trans women, that we are reinforcing gender stereotypes with how we express ourselves and thus holding back the progress of feminism. But identifying within the binary is not inherently problematic when it's done through the vehicle of self-care, which is what transition is ultimately about for many of us: healing ourselves from the trauma of dysphoria and moving forward into the positive embrace of who we truly want to be.

Besides, a cis woman embracing her womanhood is not "reinforcing the binary." To "reinforce" implies an act of coercion, that you're telling everyone, "What I'm doing is good and natural and should be done by everyone else." But identifying as a normal, boring, perhaps even stereotypically feminine woman can be done without erasing the identities of people outside the binary, without placing the binary on a normative pedestal, without transphobia, and without misogyny.

Ultimately, I don't think there's a right or wrong answer here with regard to the Bornstein vs Boylan debate. Identifying as a tranny/trap/third gender and so on is not problematic if it's done in the embrace of authenticity. But rejecting that label as inappropriate for oneself is perfectly fine. And thus we arrive at the principle: thou shalt not third-gender anyone without their express permission. Just because I define my identity in terms of my trans status, that doesn't mean someone else has to as well— they might prefer thinking of their trans experience as that of a private medical condition and not an Ur-identity.[9]

We should be focusing on listening to each other, listening to our unique stories, and celebrating our differences rather than trying to fix all trans people into a single theoretical model.

Why not let 1000 flowers bloom?

4

BECOMING THE WOMAN I NEVER WAS

When a caterpillar wraps itself in its cocoon it more or less dissolves into a goo, out of which emerges a butterfly. Is the butterfly the same entity as the caterpillar that existed pre-goo? Or is the butterfly a whole new entity? It's natural to think of the butterfly as a new creation that sprung forth from the goo. With this view, the caterpillar didn't turn into a butterfly, the caterpillar died and the butterfly was born anew.

A contrasting idea is that when an acorn turns into a tree it does not die. It merely grows from the inherent potential within itself. We say the acorn developed into the tree just like a child develops into an adult.

Are trans people more like butterflies or acorns? I relate much more to the butterfly than I do the acorn. But many trans folks relate more to the acorn. The experiences of trans people are incredibly diverse. The question isn't about which is the "correct" account: acorns or butterflies. Both are right for different people in different contexts.

The acorns of the trans world are the people who were sure of their identity from a very young age. Many of these same trans people ascribe to the "born this way" narrative where they focus strongly on genetic and biological explanations of their trans identity that place the emphasis on it being innate, a fundamental part of who they are since birth.

Acorns conform to what is sometimes called the "classic" trans narrative. It is the narrative most cis people are familiar with. This, of course, isn't the fault of trans people themselves. But the history of gatekeeping itself enacted a selection mechanism that made the acorn narrative more commonly presented in gender identity clinics.

What I am about to say is controversial within the trans community, so keep in mind that I am only speaking for myself. As a butterfly, I feel for all intents and purposes that I was a man before I discovered my trans identity and began the momentous process of transition. I performed the social role well and this performance did not conflict with my identity, which was that of a man for a long time. I was, however, a gender non-conforming male who had a feminine side I had been exploring from a young age. I played with this juxtaposition for many years until my marriage ended in my late 20s and an opportunity for further gender exploration opened up.

The more I explored my femininity, the more I realized desires were emerging that told me I could no longer live a dual life. I needed to make a binary transition to the other side of the gender spectrum. The shift in identity was largely because our society makes it very difficult for a male-identified person to make a complete social/physical/presentational transition while still holding onto their male identity. There is hardly a conceptual framework for that possibility. Nor does it sound appealing—I cherish my femme identity and have found community with femmes. It is not something I'd give up easily. That it took me 28 years to discover myself is humbling. What else have I yet to learn?

Like it or not we live in a binarist culture where manhood and womanhood are associated with certain stereotypes. I began to realize that I wanted nothing to do with these associations.

Replacing all the testosterone in your body with estrogen is an interesting exercise in experimental biology. I cried more in the first year of hormone therapy than I had the prior ten years as a creature numbed by testosterone.

Social transition provided an opportunity to learn about systemic oppression and taught me solidarity with folks of all stripes. My eyes were opened up to how fucked up this world is and how oppression really functions in this society.

My loss of male privilege gave me new a new epistemic and moral perspective from which to analyze the world. Direct exposure to rampant transphobia gave me insight into the power structures that are actively working to marginalize people.

Transition made me aware of what it's like to fear walking down the street by yourself. It taught me to fear men. In so many ways, transition has changed my entire political and social worldview. I went from being one of the most privileged people on this planet to someone who can now understand what solidarity really means.

But transition also was the catalyst for my metaphormosis. Transition turned my male identity into a goo out of which emerged a woman. I relate to the butterfly because I don't like to focus on the innate factors that predisposed me to explore femininity in the first place. I prefer instead to focus on the non-innate factors that led to the breakdown of my male identity and provided the matrix through which my trans identity developed. The whole idea of traits being "innate" is deeply problematic though. It's completely trite to insist on an interaction between nature and nurture but that's the honest truth—the trick is figuring out the relative contribution.

I worry that the "born this way" narrative is dangerous fodder for conservatives and bigots hellbent on trans genocide. If we find a biological cause of trans identity, would some parents screen and terminate their babies if they thought they'd turn out trans? After all, many people see it as a medical condition or disorder of some kind—I have seen trans people I love struggle with suicide as a result of their intense dysphoria. Whether its a psychiatric disorder or endocrinological disorder doesn't matter—if it's a disorder of any kind why wouldn't people try to eradicate it from our species?

This is one of the reasons why I prefer to focus on the non-biological factors at play in the formation of my own trans identity. As Preciado puts it, "Why change your mood when you can change identities?"[10] Obviously, there were some biological factors at play because it's certainly true that a complex trait like a trans identity (powerful enough to cause transition) is always going to be a mixture of both nature and nurture. But in so many trans narratives we see a reluctance to talk about the nurture side of the equation. There is a fear that if we admit such factors people will either think we're phonies or that we can just go to therapy to cure ourselves of the desire to transition.

I reject both claims. Just because there are non-biological factors at play does not mean conversion therapy will work. The presence of non-biological factors does not mean we can just consciously choose to be trans. The question of "is it a choice" is oversimplified because we have to distinguish between unconscious and conscious cognitive processes that make decisions. The unconscious feeds off many non-biological factors, just as the conscious system does. The existence of choice, therefore, does not mean it's willy-nilly and can just be consciously overridden.

Take, for example, doctors: nobody is born with a "doctor gene." But obviously if you choose to be a doctor that doesn't make you a phony doctor. Similarly, there is probably not a single "trans gene." But choosing to transition doesn't make you a phony woman. It's the performance of doctorhood that makes you a doctor and it's the performance of womanhood that counts—women are made, not born, as Simone de Beauvoir famously said. We must understand that "performing womanhood" is not the same as performing femininity. You can violate every stereotype known and still perform womanhood authentically because the important thing is the identification process.

And once you perform a role long enough it becomes automatized, habitualized, unconscious, and thus "natural." It becomes part of the unconscious schemas that structure your total personality.

While in many ways I am still quite similar to the man I once was, in many more ways I am a new person. Going on the classic Lockean model[11] of personal identity, there are enough significant psychological discontinuities with who I once was to warrant thinking I am a whole new person. I have become the woman I never was.

Going on the butterfly model, for me it feels more accurate that I was not a woman born into the body of a man but rather a man who turned into a woman. I was not a woman peering out from behind the eyes of a male. I was a gender non-conforming male who had a complex set of new desires emerge from a period of intense gender exploration in my 20s. These included a desire for a feminine name, she/her pronouns, hormone therapy, laser treatment, and more or less a complete change in appearance.

My sexual desires also changed. I went from being bi-curious to pansexual (though still leaning heavily towards women and preferring women for long-term domestic partnership).

All my feelings about my body changed. I did not have significantly intense gender dysphoria before I realized that I needed to transition. Transition brought my gender dysphoria up from the depths of my unconscious. Thus, from a phenomenological perspective it seems that it was not gender dysphoria that caused transition but transition that caused dysphoria. When I came to the realization I wanted to transition, I began to understand this would not be an easy pathway because my body, face, and voice would make it difficult to relieve the social aspect of gender dysphoria, which involves people seeing me as a woman.

Again, I want to emphasize that my phenomenology might not be true of all trans people. We all have our own stories, our own life history, and what's true for me might not be true for anyone else. But I think we do a disservice to ourselves by focusing too much on acorns while ignoring butterflies. Both are beautiful. Both are valid. And there are probably hybrid acorn-butterflies and everything in-between. The trans community is diverse and the cis media has only begun to understand us.

5

EMBRACING AMBIGUITY

When I get right down to it, I am a mixture, a blend of both the masculine and the feminine. I have long hair but a deep(ish) voice, smooth skin but an adam's apple, small breasts but broad shoulders, full lips but an angular jaw, plucked eyebrows and a large nose.

I wear makeup while my face can be androgynous. I wear women's clothing while being tall and muscular. I am a contradiction. An anomaly. I challenge people's expectations every day. Who is this person before you who looks like a woman but sounds like a man? Why does that woman have a prominent adam's apple? Why are her arms so muscular and her hands so big? Why is her hairline so high?

I can't tell you how many times I've been at work and had customers—usually little children—debate among themselves what my gender is. Kids are never quite sure. And I often observe adults struggling with pronouns around me; there is a slight sense of hesitation, they are not quite sure if I'm a "he" or "she," and they offer one suggestion quietly, tentatively, and then watch for my reaction. I am stoic—I have learned to not react either way because I never want to be accused of "tricking" anyone. I'm just trying to be myself.

Like most trans women, I often feel as if passing is everything. Most of us strive for more of it, whatever "it" means (usually a moving target). More blendability. Greater capacity for going stealth. Less ambiguity. More fitting in. Not violating expectations. Safety. Avoiding being misgendered. Fighting social dysphoria.

Many if not most of us strive for "it" but few trans women ever get to 100 percent passability. In my experience, there's usually something about us that makes us clockable on closer inspection. For trans women, this is often our voices.

So what do we do? We have to cope somehow. Regardless of whether we pass we still have to go out into the world and buy groceries, run errands, go to the doctor, and do all the other mundane tasks that involve interacting with strangers. We have to strengthen ourselves to accept the reality of our situation because the only other option is paralysis or death. I try to accept that I will never live up perfectly to the cis-normative standard for what a Woman™ is "supposed" to be like. Maybe one day I will afford to have my trachea shaved down. Or maybe one day I will be able to find professional voice therapy covered by insurance. But for now, I need to come up with practical coping strategies to deal with the fact that I don't pass 100 percent and yet I still have to live my life.

One such coping strategy is to embrace ambiguity as an inevitable but ultimately not-so-bad reality, to embrace the idea of confusing people, of challenging people's expectations of what it means to be a woman (or a man). As Bornstein put it, "It's frightening to be genderless. What makes it easier is a sense of humor."[12] Or going even further, challenging the notion of what it means to be a person in today's modern society where gender transition is a real phenomenon. The specter of transition now raises the question of transhumanism: how has technology—in this case *gender* technology—altered what it means to be human?

Although I would prefer to be gendered correctly and seen as a "normal" woman (at least until people get to know me in which case I'm happy to depart from convention—the desire for normalcy is more about making a first impression), I know this is not going to happen all the time. So how do I cope?

In order to embrace my own ambiguity, I have been trying to develop the attitude of (1) not giving a fuck and (2) embracing my androgyny as a positive trait. Some people are actually attracted to androgyny so I tell myself that even if I don't pass 100 percent it doesn't make me less attractive or valid. Some people like mixtures, blends, syntheses, amalgamations, fusions. At the very least I can go for the "alien femme" aesthetic you sometimes see in the entertainment industry.

Some enjoy the fact that my body is a contradiction, a field on which competing elements battle. This knowledge of my body being ideal to some people is a great comfort because when I get into a relationship it helps dispel my fear that they're just going to abandon me for a cis partner with a more congenial arrangement of body parts.

Many men are attracted to trans women specifically because of their trans status, a polite way of saying: they like chicks with dicks. In the community, these men are called "chasers." I have never liked that term because it erases the possibility of a category of people who are specifically attracted to trans people in the same way some people have a "thing" for brunettes without that attraction being fetishistic, objectifying, focused on body parts, or otherwise too problematic. I call these people "trans amorous." And it's not just men. Cis women (and trans people) can be trans amorous as well but I think women are socialized to be more polite about it whereas men are overly blunt. I have heard some men express their attraction to trans women not in terms of our body parts but in terms of their comfort with us as women who have, perhaps, more insight into male psychology having lived among them, like an anthropologist who went native.

My other coping strategy besides embracing ambiguity is indirect. It's through relationships and friendships in both my personal and professional life. If I am in a relationship or friendship and that person has only known me as Rachel, it really helps appease the demons of dysphoria because I see them unconsciously using "she/her" pronouns. The "unconscious," or habitual, nature of pronoun usage is validating because it's what happens when people get to know me as a person—it comes naturally.

And that's a good feeling. It says: I see you. I know you. You are valid. Don't worry about your ambiguity. It's ok. I like you and see your womanhood as valid, despite how deep your voice is, despite how muscular you are, and so on. Building up a social circle of people who automatically gender me female has been an important part of my self-actualization. This is why I enjoy hanging out with trans people. They usually have an above-average ability to correctly gender people regardless of what they look like or how they present themselves. Most cis people seem to struggle with this and rely on superficial physical cues to orient their gender frameworks.

So in a nutshell, my strategy is to embrace ambiguity. To relish it. Will this strategy completely dispel my dysphoria and social anxiety? No, not really. That's too much to ask. But it's another weapon in my arsenal.

6

ON BEING AN ANGRY TRANNY

I wasn't always an angry tranny.

And yes, the correct term is "tranny," not "trans woman" or "trans person." It's angry *tranny* because when transphobes see a trans woman getting upset over some social justice issue they are not thinking, "Oh those darn trans women are so upset." They're thinking to themselves, "Fucking trannies, always getting their panties in a twist," "Tranny SJWs are so predictable," and so on.

The slur is part and parcel of being an angry tranny and the image of the "angry tranny SJW" has taken on a cultural momentum of meme-like proportions. The "angry tranny" stereotype has a long history, made famous in the Stonewall riots, where it's reported that a trans woman threw the first bricks, kicking off the historical fight for LGBT+ rights.

When Andi Dier, a trans woman, recently confronted Rose McGowan at a book tour about some transphobic statements made on RuPaul's podcast, the eventual escalation into shouting was later interpreted by many in terms of the archetype of the angry tranny, the tranny activist, and so on. According to the archetype, the angry tranny gets irrationally and aggressively or "mannishly" upset over some trivial thing that is blown up under the auspices of "trans misogyny." According to the stereotype, the angry tranny is never justified in her righteous anger—it's always interpreted as a manifestation of male privilege.

And it would be naive to think that trans women never live up to the stereotype. I did listen to the Dier confrontation and to me she did come across as pretty aggressive, especially since she was being aggressive towards another woman, a rape survivor nonetheless. I personally would not use a confrontational tone in that kind of context and prefer to make connection always with the possibility of fundamental reform. If I am "calling someone out," I want to make sure I never lose my sense of solidarity. McGowan might have said some trans-misogynistic things but I prefer personally to use a "softer" approach in these kinds of close, interpersonal exchanges, especially when there is trauma involved.[13]

Women of color, especially trans women of color, have been behind every major civil rights issue since forever. They are the original agitators. For trans women, the refusal to obey the rules assigned to them by a cis-sexist patriarchal society agitates the inner gears of the gender machine, the all-encompassing system of norms, unwritten rules, scripts, stereotypes, and so on that defines our existence in a human society and feeds off all human difference.

Trans women everywhere and especially those with intersecting identities have good reasons to be pissed off at all kinds of fucked-up shit in our society. One of the functions behind the modern concept of being "woke" is that when you become aware of how oppressive power works in one domain of marginalization it becomes much easier to see how destructive systems of oppression, discrimination, exploitation, corruption, prejudice, and violence exist along other axes of identity.

In other words, once you understand the logic behind, for example, systemic racism, it's easier to feel solidarity with all other marginalized folks in a way that is attuned to how marginalization happens on the institutional level. It's one thing to understand how things like racism and sexism work on isolated individual examples; it's quite another to see and feel how the whole system is rigged against those on the margins. This is why trans women are so often agitated about the "Whole Damn System" and are stereotyped to be such fierce social justice advocates.

And it's not just gender. The whole economic-social system is corrupt—capitalism doesn't escape the ire of the angry tranny. Once you start unraveling the failures of the trans healthcare system, you also start tugging on threads involving universal healthcare, income inequality, and the dangers of the boom-and-bust cycles of capitalism. When you understand how the pathologization of trans identities depends on using insurance to gain access to medical transition resources and then tie that into how the current insurance system in America is itself a failed product of the capitalist system, it's easy to see how systemic transphobia intersects with the economic realities of capitalism. To put it concretely, when you need a $30,000 surgery to treat your debilitating gender dysphoria and you are making $9 an hour at the local coffee shop, anger at the transphobic jerk who harassed you yesterday is easily sublated into anger at all the intersecting systems of power that created the neuroses of modern society.

I wasn't always this angry. Transition slowly changed how I viewed the world. It changed my internal moral life and gave me the perspective to understand the concept of solidarity with folks living in oppressive systems. It expanded my capacity for empathy. I went from literally being one of the most privileged people on the planet to someone with a whole lot more to lose by remaining silent about social injustice.

I can no longer afford to be cordial, intellectual, rarified, and theoretical in my direct discourse. As an academic philosopher, I spent a lot of time hanging out with white cis straight males who have a tendency to treat pressing social problems as curious thought experiments. They debate social issues like an intellectual debate, a game of wit and logical acumen. Trans people are seen as "interesting" because we present problems for the metaphysics of gender and identity. Determining the boundaries of consent for harassment is an intellectual game, not a lived experience like it is for so many women.

The question for me used to be, "Who has the cleverest argument?" but now my instinct leans towards, "Who is this hurting?" This general shift from curiosity to empathy has created a new paradigm through which to view the problems of social justice. Transition "woke" me to the fucked-up reality of being a marginalized person. And I don't even have it that bad! All in all, I live a good life and I am not all doom and gloom about my own prospects for living a good life. But, my daily existence as a visibly trans woman has opened my eyes to so many aspects of our society that, when considered in full reflection, can only give rise to righteous anger.

This is not to say there are no other emotions involved besides anger. Fear, shame, disgust, and sadness come to mind when thinking about my reaction to systemic transphobia.

Other trans women have talked about how having a "feminist awakening" is a common phenomenon during transition. It's not surprising that being a target of harassment, violence, hate and governmental regulation concerning what you do with your body will make you a more stringent feminist when bodily autonomy has always been a central cornerstone of women's movements.

So many white cis people use the stereotype of the angry tranny, the angry feminist, the angry woman of color, to invalidate our experiences, our analysis, our solutions. But until all systems of oppression are eradicated, I will remain angry, agitated, and antagonistic. As Audre Lorde so correctly put it, "My fear of anger taught me nothing. Your fear of that anger will teach you nothing, also."[14]

FEMINIST MUSINGS

7

TRANS FEMINISM IS REAL FEMINISM

Trans feminism sometimes gets mistaken as feminism's little cousin, a mere side show to the Main Event: Cis Feminism, i.e. feminism written by and for other cis women.

On a superficial level, this seems fitting. After all, 99 percent of women on this planet are cis so it makes sense that "feminism" is largely concerned with the perspective of cis women. According to this logic, "trans feminism" is merely "feminism light," a pale shadow of the real thing.

In contrast to cis feminism, intersectional feminism strives to incorporate the insights of *all* women, cis or trans, straight or gay, disabled or able-bodied, black or white. The idea is that if you are a black woman the oppression you face as a *black* woman intersects with the oppression you face as a black *woman*. Gender and race also intersect with socio-economic status, disability, sexual orientation, and so on.

Being trans is just another axis along which intersectionality functions. Any feminism worth its weight recognizes this. Trans women have experiences that overlap with cis women as well as experiences that don't. But that's not inherently different from black women having experiences that overlap or don't overlap with those of white women.

Not only is trans feminism real feminism, real feminism *must* incorporate the insights of trans feminism if it is to be complete, to the extent any feminism can ever be complete. If you are a cis person, I can already feel your reluctance: why must the 99 percent include the 1 percent? The answer is not that feminism must accept *this* particular 1 percent, but rather, feminism must be able to absorb *all* the "1 percents." It's not just about trans women. But trans women represent a litmus test—as women prematurely assigned "male" at birth, if feminism can accept *us*, including other "kinds" of women should be easy. As Audre Lorde wrote, "It is not our differences that divide us. It is our inability to recognize, accept, and celebrate those differences."[1]

In my opinion it's a fool's game to try and find the experience or set of experiences that is universal among all women. But that doesn't imply that the concept "woman" is without meaning. Philosophers have noted that it is surprisingly difficult to give necessary and sufficient conditions for simple concepts like "chair," yet I know a chair when I see one. In a way, this is similar to when Supreme Court Justice Potter Stewart couldn't define the difference between porn and erotic art, but famously said, "I know it when I see it." I can't define "womanhood" but I know it when I see it.

Why should we expect complex concepts like "woman" to have simple definitions? I might not be able to define womanhood precisely in such a way that will correctly sort billions of unique individuals into two mutually exclusive classes: women and not-women. It's not so easy! Yet I know a woman when I see one. And "seeing" here is, of course, a metaphor for understanding. A pre-transition trans woman can radiate her womanhood without necessarily "passing" as a woman. "Passing" as a cis woman is such an arbitrary standard anyway, because there are cis women who get misgendered on a regular basis.

Why will feminism never be complete without the inclusion of trans people? Because feminism has inputs. It's not just done completely a priori. It operates with experiences and narratives as data to be explained. Traditional feminism started with only the experiences of white middle-class women as the inputs and got quite a bit done. But it was far from complete. Then black feminists started feeding in their inputs. And through similar processes, the voices of people from diverse backgrounds have given their inputs.

Trans people represent 1 percent of the population. That might not sounds like a lot but that's millions and millions of data points. And furthermore, they are data points that are highly relevant to feminism in so far as trans people have unique insights into the dynamics of gender that should be of special interest to feminist theory. So not only does trans feminism bring the experience of millions of trans women, trans men, and non-binary folks, it brings it in a way that has the potential to reshape the very concepts central to feminism.

Some prominent feminist theorists such as Judith Butler have recognized the radical potential of trans theory and have started to work through those insights. And, of course, trans feminists themselves have been dissecting this stuff for decades (see the Further Resources section at the end of the book).

But feminism has yet to fully digest the trans experience. Though a mere "1 percent," trans folks have so much to bring to feminism, with spectacular proclivity to keep pressuring feminism to remain intersectional.

As intersectional feminists, it's easy to believe our feminism is fully intersectional yet so often we fall short. To me, it seems the best tactic is to remain humble about the intersectional reach of our feminism. There are probably voices feminism has yet to hear, or voices that we have heard but not heard *deeply*. I try to keep in mind that my writing will always be imperfect, that I inevitably view the world from a limited point of view. My feminism will never be complete. But it is that very incompleteness which encourages me to keep learning and listening.

Any feminism without trans experience is partially blind. This is why trans feminism is real feminism. Real feminism is spongelike in its absorption of different perspectives. Any feminism that fails to uptake the experience of trans people is incomplete at best and actively harmful at worst.

But the point is not that the inclusion of trans people absolutely needs to be the number one priority of feminism. Rather, the point is that we should be strengthening our intersectional muscles *in general*, and listening to trans people is a fantastic exercise. If cis feminism can include trans feminism, feminism itself is in a good position to be more intersectional in all areas of life.

8

THE PARADOXICAL DUALITY OF CAT-CALLING AS A TRANS WOMAN

The other night I was cat-called. I was walking back out to my car at a gas station and there was a group of young males standing around outside the store. Reading the situation, I was extremely on edge, sensing in their oozing machismo the possibility of them either leering at me (making it more likely for me to be clocked) or for them to start talking to me (making it more likely I would have to use my voice which would possibly out me as not-quite-what-I-seemed).

One of them calls out, "Hey sweetheart, how's it going?"

Do I say something? Can I get away with just ignoring them? What if they get more insistent with a stronger follow-up? What if my ignoring them makes them angry? But if I say something then I have to use my voice, which is deeper in pitch with a lower resonance than than they are probably expecting. I still have no idea how it reads to other people. Sometimes I pass over the phone, other times I don't. It's a gamble.

Many feelings rushed through me as I finally muttered softly, "I'm good" while attempting to get in my car as fast as possible.

One of the feelings I felt most strongly was fear. I was afraid that my voice would enable them to clock me, and the man who cat-called me, having clocked me, or having his friends clock me, would feel his fragile little sense of masculinity was threatened and then proceed to beat the shit out of me for trying to "trick" him into being "gay," hence getting into my car as fast as possible.

Another feeling was disgust. I was disgusted at how piggish men can be towards people they read as "fuckable" and felt a twinge of injustice in solidarity with other woman-identified people who get cat-called on a regular basis.

But here is the paradoxical feeling the title of this essay alluded to: in addition to fear and disgust, I also felt a boost to my self-esteem because being cat-called is an indication that people perceive me to be female, or at least female enough to be deemed worthy of the male gaze. Since my own dysphoria is at least partly based on how other people react to me, and my goal in transition is to get misgendered less and affirmed in my gender more, it's paradoxical in so far as the cat-calling was positive evidence in favor of strangers reading me as an attractive woman.

I have seen TERFs talk about this as another example of why trans women have male privilege and don't understand what it's like to be a woman: according to them we *like* being cat-called and thus cannot understand the oppressive nature of male harassment. But that's not true at all.

The encounter was for me paradoxical precisely because it contained within itself competing elements of fear/disgust *and* a positive feeling of gender euphoria at evidence of "passing" as my identified gender. It's not that I liked being cat-called—I was afraid of being beaten up or worse and my deep feminist intuitions scream at the horribleness of cat-calling as a phenomenon that negatively affects women. If I had had a choice, I would have not experienced the encounter at all because the small positive of affirmation is not worth the greater negative of fear and disgust.

It's not so simple as either liking it or not liking it. But I would be lying if I said that I had zero positive feelings at being cat-called—the negative feelings were mixed into the positive feeling of gender euphoria, at feeling as if I am both passing and attractive.

In my casual conversations with cis women about this topic, many of them also feel the paradoxical feeling as well, for example feeling as if their outfit and hair must be killing it today because they got cat-called which is unusual for them but also feeling disgusted at the misogyny on display and also feeling fear.

But I would also wager that for trans women the paradox is felt to a greater extent. For many trans woman, including myself, passing is of great importance and sometimes it's difficult to garner "objective" evidence that you are passing. Cat-calling is a form of evidence and thus brings with it a positive feeling. Nevertheless, we need to do a better job of raising young men to also feel disgust at the practice of cat-calling and to call-out and shame fellow men for doing it when they see it.

9

DYSPHORIA AS A SYMPTOM OF MODERNITY

Dysphoria is everywhere we look in American society. Take, for example, the toxic beauty culture that women everywhere are forced to take part in. Part of this culture involves the media promoting images of beautiful, highly photoshopped models representing unattainable ideals, often whitewashed with the assumption that lighter-skinned = better; small waist and big tits = better; long, fine hair (also known as white hair) = better, and so on.

Dysphoria, in a nutshell, is special kind of discomfort, an amorphous, many-headed feeling that something is *not quite right*. There are many young women wishing they were skinnier, with bigger breasts, and the right size ass (big is "in" right now but not *too* big and certainly not fat-big but rather big as a result of doing 200 squat thrusts—and lord forbid you have *cellulite*), with different hair, or different hips (without stretch marks), hating their skin, or their nose, or a whole litany of body parts that don't adequately match what they see in music videos.

I would imagine many if not most girls and women in America wish they could change something about their bodies or appearance. And not just occasionaly thinking, "Oh, that would be nice"—I'm talking about near-obessive fixation on how much better their life would be if only [insert body part] was different. Men and boys have their own "beauty culture" as well, although it would be better called an "anti-beauty" culture, defined by Old Spice commercials, Marvel superheroes, and the strongly enforced norm that caring about your appearance = gay. Men have to find that perfect balance of not looking *too* much like a slob but also not being "prissy" about their appearance.

We live in a fix-it society exemplified by reality TV shows depicting "ugly" people getting a smorgasbord of cosmetic surgeries and then showing the dramatic "before and after" reveal. The plastic surgery industry is a multi-billion growth bonanza—with surgeons making big bucks by not having to deal with medical insurance, just straight up cash, please and thank you. But dysphoria is at the core of this phenomenon, a cultural dysphoria we have all internalized due to our exposure to unrealistic beauty ideals and constant exposure to a digitally altered world where thick Instagram filters hide the fact that a normal person's face is not a perfectly smooth mask.

There are many flavors and varieties of dysphoria—and it is not just a transgender thing either. It just means discomfort about some aspect of yourself or how that aspect is perceived by others. But dysphoria is probably more associated these days with gender dysphoria.

Gender dysphoria is a special kind of dysphoria that is felt when you are uncomfortable in your body because it either makes you feel like the wrong gender or makes you socially perceived as the wrong gender. Gender dysphoria has been scientifically studied for decades and has historical precedents dating back hundreds if not thousands of years.

Many kinds of treatment are available to gender dysphoric people. Therapy. Hormones. Sexual reassignment. Plastic surgery. These treatments are effective, both life-affirming and life-saving. I do not think these treatments necessarily have to be seen through a "medical" lens, like fixing a broken arm. I think the medical framework is appropriate and useful in many cases, but not all.

For some trans people, these treatments are more about affirming their lived experience and being true to themselves than correcting some horrible pathology. It's about *finally* seeing yourself in a mirror, something cis people take for granted. We do not *have* to buy into any system of thought that sees all trans people as these broken creatures in need of fixing with the doctor's help. Some trans people might think they are broken but other trans people are actually *glad* to be trans. Where do you ever hear about that in the cis media?

I now want to step back and ask a bigger question: why is dysphoria a symptom of *modern* society? My hypothesis is that dysphoria is a symptom of the hyper-sexualizing, beauty-obsessed modern media machine that is Hollywood and American media at large, either in video games or magazines, or the models we see on the walls of every department store. It's everywhere. When you see perfection every day it's hard to not feel as if, well, if I had the money to spare, maybe I really *would* like to have perfect teeth, or bigger breasts, or fewer wrinkles around my eyes, or a flat stomach. If I had I these things, then I would look younger, better, newer, improved, and surely happiness would follow, right?

We might be tempted to make an analogy with trans people to explain this beauty-based form of dysphoria. We might think that "facial feminization surgery" for trans women is essentially just cosmetic surgery that reduces masculine features and emphasizes feminine features. The analogy is tempting because the dysphoria of a cis woman wanting plastic surgery to look presumably more feminine and beautiful *seems* an awful lot like that of a trans woman wanting plastic surgery to look more feminine. Metaphysically they seem to be very similar.

But we must be careful with this analogy. Very careful, because we can make a distinction between healthy and non-healthy kinds of dysphoria, strange as that sounds at first blush. What kind of dysphoria would be healthy? First and foremost, the kind that can be treated. If the underlying cause is rooted in gender, then there are proven treatments that often lead to easing the burden of gender dysphoria, though it might be present at low background levels or in intermittent bursts. Second, in cultures that have a recognized social role for gender expansive people, the kind of dysphoria present in those populations is not necessarily unhealthy so long as society at large approves of transition and has the mechanisms in place to ensure transition happens smoothly.

However, the kind of dysphoria that stems from trying to live up to the beauty ideals in media and culture is a lot harder to treat because it's based on a flawed ideology, an ideology of the body, an ideology of what the body is supposed to be. This is also the root of cis normativity as well. This kind of dysphoria is hard to treat with technology because the problem actually lies in the culture at large, not necessarily in the individual. The media machine that spreads unattainable beauty ideals into every aspect of society is unstoppable and getting worse as our appetite as conspicuous consumers grows larger. I don't see it going away anytime soon. This affects everyone, but especially young women.

Men have their own unique kind of dysphoria surrounding things like going bald, muscles, penis size, testosterone levels, career pathways, social standing, and so on. They see physically perfect super-men in Marvel movies and feel inspired to get a superhero body but few ever get to that level, just like most women don't look like Kim Kardashian. Couple the widespread prevalence of muscle-bound male models and celebrities with the toxic masculinity of machismo culture and you have a recipe for boys and men feeling dysphoric about their bodies. The difference, however, is that it's considered socially acceptable (and even desirable) for men to have "dad bods," which is another way of basically holding women to incredibly high standards of physical beauty while giving men a free pass because everyone knows dads are lazy, lovable slobs, right?

But I think it is these media-driven kinds of dysphoria that are unhealthy and thus different from the healthiness of gender dysphoria, which is rooted in the concept of gender, a concept that is both fluid and fundamental to our essence as people. In contrast, the beauty ideals of society are not core essential features of humanity—we can do without them just fine.

Last, and this is important, I do not want to judge any particular person for getting cosmetic surgery, or spending $300 a month at Sephora (so long as they're not going into debt). I support the autonomy of rational people to make decisions about their bodies as they see fit. And who am I to judge—there are definitely some cosmetic procedures I'd go for immediately if I had the money (e.g. my nose is long and slightly crooked and drives me crazy and my boobs are really small). But surely there are some cosmetic surgeries that cannot be described as healthy. People get talked into more work being done by overly enthusiastic surgeons during consultation. That tenth nosejob because the last one just wasn't quite perfect *might* not be entirely healthy. Maybe.

10

SAPIOSEXUALISM IS HERE TO STAY

If you have gone on any internet dating app lately you've probably noticed the term "sapiosexual" in people's profile. Most people use this to mean they are highly attracted to and turned on by intelligence. Seems innocent enough. But if you go on leftist Facebook groups making fun of people's dating profiles, you'll see that in leftist politics right now it's almost universally agreed that saying you are a sapiosexual is a Bad Thing and immediately outs you as not being "woke."

The origins of "sapiosexualism" as a concept date back to 1998 when Livejournal user "wolfieboy" coined the term to describe his sexual attraction. In a 2002 post he writes:[2] "I don't care too much about the plumbing. I want an incisive, inquisitive, insightful, irreverent mind. I want someone for whom philosophical discussion is foreplay." In other words, wolfieboy seems to be a bi/pan person who loves philosophy, which in itself seems fairly innocuous.

So why has sapiosexualism become the target of so much leftist backlash? In modern "woke" circles, identifying as a sapiosexual is almost certainly bound to induce cringing.

The argument goes that sapiosexualism is a form of ableism because you are judging people with different mental abilities as being less valid and ignoring the neurodiversity of differently abled people. These leftists argue along intersectional grounds that sapiosexualism tends to focus on only a single narrow type of intelligence at the expense of other equally valid modes of being. This narrow type is the MENSA-esque type that is good at logic puzzles and doing math in their head, who score high on IQ tests and other tests of "raw cognitive power," as psychologists put it.

But IQ is just one "form" of intelligence. Think of a musical or artistic genius with a gift for imaginative thought, who may not necessarily have a high IQ but whose mind is brimming with interesting and creative ideas. IQ does have some correlation with creativity but in general they represent two different cognitive systems and one does not necessarily imply the other.

Why are people attracted to intelligence though? Sexual selection is an established mechanism for evolutionary change and useful for understanding sapiosexualism. In essence, what members of a species find sexually attractive in a mate can exert a selection pressure for that trait. A classic example is the ornate plumage of birds. If the females of a species all are more attracted to one style of plumage (e.g. ornateness), then there will be competition within the males and adaptive pressures will begin to work. In cases like the peacock, the preference for "more ornate is better" can lead to runaway selection that works against the survival of the individual as the heavy tail weighs them down when flying away from a potential predator. But the reproductive pay-off is worth the trade-off in survival, otherwise it would not have been selected for.

Some evolutionary researchers have hypothesized that IQ is a trait that has been under sexual selection. The idea goes that humans prefer other humans with high IQs because high IQs are correlated with higher problem-solving ability, which is obviously relevant to surviving and being able to provide calories and protection to offspring. However, some researchers have also hypothesized that creativity, for example storytelling or musical abilities, could have been sexually selected for as a proxy for IQ (problem-solving survival ability). If this were true, it would explain why surveys of people asking for their top preferred traits in mating partners consistently rank intelligence and humor at the top. Kindness is up there as well. Intelligence and kindness make sense in terms of how they can affect the success of offspring. But humor? That can only be explained by sexual selection.

Now that we understand the basics of sexual selection, we can understand why sapiosexualism is both perfectly normally and acceptable but also ableist and short-sighted.

The key is to look more closely at the *type* of intelligence most self-proclaimed "sapiosexuals" value. As I said above, usually this means the type of intelligence associated with getting good scores on "intelligence tests." But intelligence tests are only a narrow slice of human cognitive function. From an operational perspective, having a high score on an IQ test can *only* mean that you are good at taking IQ tests. It says nothing about your ability to solve real-world problems, your wisdom, or your emotional and social intelligence.

Someone might be a "slow thinker" when compared with someone with a high IQ but often that slow turning of thoughts, that mulling-over process, can lead to tremendous insight. In a fast-paced world sometimes a slower, more reflective approach can generate outside-the-box solutions to otherwise intractable problems. This is why we often get our best ideas when we are sleeping, that is, when our unconscious brains are filtering through the day's information and solving our problems for us.

Furthermore, sexual selection itself shows that being attracted to intelligence is so much more than just being attracted to people who are good at taking intelligence tests. The dynamics of interpersonal mate selection are *way* more complicated than that. Kindness, humor, empathy, emotional intelligence, charisma, morality, wisdom, patience, creativity—these are some of the traits relevant to sexual selection besides just "quick thinking."

Another problem with sapiosexualism is how it advertises itself within the context of dating profiles: as a sexual orientation. Right there beside "gay," "straight," and "pansexual" is "sapiosexual," misleadingly indicating that attraction to intelligence constitutes an entirely new axis along which we can think about sexual orientation. But this fundamentally misconstrues the domain of sexual orientation, which is about *gender*. Sapiosexualism has more to do with *relationship compatibility* than it does *orientation*. Because the thing is, most of the self-identified sapiosexuals out there, many of them straight cis men, would probably not date a super smart person who did not at least meet their bare minimum standards of attractiveness. This is why a preference for smart people is not an entire orientation unto itself.

I want to say more about relationship compatibility. For me personally, the type of intelligence associated with a "cerebral" university education is important in long-term relationship compatibility. This is because I simply enjoy talking about certain domains of inquiry, philosophy, science, politics, and so on, and I simply could not be in a long-term relationship with someone who utterly failed to find those things interesting. This is not to say we have to have an exact set of overlapping intellectual interests. But it is important to me to at least *have* an intellectual curiosity about the world, not because having that makes one a better person, but simply because that's the conversational style I prefer to have with my partners.

I *like* abstract philosophical thought experiments. I *like* discussing the results of scientific studies. I *like* talking the mechanics of political science. My preference for dating someone who shares those interests does not seem inherently to be a value judgment on those who are either not interested or not capable of being interested in those things. It's simply a dating preference, like a professional athlete being interested in dating someone who is also active and into sports.

And before you say that I am missing the full diversity of human experience with such a limited dating preference, I have actually dated people significantly less cerebral in their interests and I have enjoyed and cherished those relationships in their own way and have learned so much from them, but ultimately they were not as satisfying as the relationships where my own peculiar intellectual predilections could be appreciated and vice versa.

I am fully aware that this probably makes me seem horribly pretentious. I am ok with that. Philosophy is about as "ivory tower" as you get. But I have always enjoyed philosophy of the everyman such as the writings of people like Alan Watts, people who abhor intellectual elitism and strive to make their work accessible to everyone with the operating assumption that ordinary people living ordinary lives can be brimming with wisdom and valuable philosophical insight into the Good Life.

In the end, we are left with a compromise between those who feel that sapiosexualism is a natural extension of their sexual identity and those who feel it is pretentious, elitist, and ableist. We can appeal to evolution to explain both why sapiosexualism makes sense to people and why it is myopic in its understanding of what types of intelligence are attractive in romantic partners. Nobody should feel guilty for being attracted to people with big brains. But, at the same time, we shouldn't limit our understanding of "big brain" to only those good at taking IQ tests. There is so much more to the human mind. Furthermore, when thinking about our own attraction to intelligence, a considerable factor is which kinds of intelligence mesh well together in terms of relationship compatibility. Would an apolitical non-voter be compatible with a political junkie? Would a sports nut be compatible with someone who hates exercise? And then there is emotional intelligence, the great glue that ties relationships together. We ignore its importance at our own peril when choosing our partners (or friends).

11

WHY I WAS NOT BORN IN THE WRONG BODY

It is often said that identity is central to trans people, that our very existence is defined by our so-called "gender identity." Our identity is thus said to be central to who we are, our mode of being. But is that really true? First of all, does it have to be central? What if it was only secondary? Or tertiary? Or multi-dimensional? Second, what if our identity did not actually exist at all, at least not in the way concrete things like tigers and rivers exist?

When we say, "I was born in the wrong body," what is this "I" being referred to? And is this "I" something that exists separately from the flux of ions that is the sum of our neurobiological activity? Is it separate from the atomic flows which constitute our bodies?

But whatever it is, surely it was not the fully developed, self-reflective, autobiographical consciousness that was born in the wrong body. Because that consciousness was not born but rather grown—grown in the social matrix of our environment, our learning history, our socialization, and so on. As Simone de Beauvoir famously said, "One is not born, but rather, becomes a woman."[3]

And what exactly is this conscious identity we speak of when we talk about being trapped in the wrong body? Does it really exist or is it an illusion? Of course, illusions themselves really exist, but they exist as illusions. But who is getting tricked? Perhaps the "who" being tricked is the trick itself.

There is a real possibility that we will never be able to think about this stuff sensibly, in the same way it's almost impossible to visually imagine 12 dimensions in hyperspace. We are in the end left with metaphors. But that's not so bad. In fact, it's great because metaphor is the fundamental building block of cognition anyway. So that actually puts us in a great position to think about consciousness. Consciousness is an illusion. That's the metaphor. Or at least one metaphor. Another powerful metaphor is software running on hardware. The metaphors are endless.

Anyway, what we might mean by "trapped in the wrong body" is that the body I desire to have is different from the body that I grew up in. But what does it mean to grow up "in" a body? And it's different in a way that is fundamentally gendered. My ideal body would have never suffered so much testosterone exposure. It would have never presented itself to doctors in a way that made them declare, "It's a boy!"

Ideally, my body would have taken quite a different journey. But in so far as my current consciousness would be radically different if my history of embodiment was radically different, is it not a wish for death to wish for a different body? If I did not have my trans history, I would literally be a different person. If I truly wished to be that different person, I am wishing for the end of my current self. And thus could my "ideal" body really be ideal if I would need to die to realize it?

I am probably one of the luckier trans folks who actually does not wish to be a different person. Although there are, of course, things about myself I would change in a heartbeat, I am content with the person I am. I don't mean content in the sense that I have no room to grow and be a better person. I am not perfect by any means. But content in the sense of not wishing to be a radically different person.

If I had been "born a girl," would I have become a philosopher? Given how sexist the field of philosophy is (not to mention the society itself), it's unlikely. Yet my primary identity is that of "philosopher."[4] Before "woman," I am a philosopher. Before "trans," I am a philosopher. Being a philosopher is more predictive of my behavior and thought than any other trait. It's fundamental to who I am and how I operate.

This is the self I am content with. It is likely that if I rewound the tape of my life and started fresh with a new embodiment that I would not be who I am today.

And the person I am today is largely a happy and well-adjusted person. I have had my share of difficulties but I consider myself to be a lucky person. If I was a Christian, I would say I am "blessed." Yes, indeed, I am quite blessed to be alive. I am 31 years old and I am looking forward to the next 70 years of health, happiness, love, and knowledge. I look forward to growing into myself as a woman, as a writer, as a lover, as a friend, and as a person.

12

THE INHERENT SUPERIORITY OF SOFTNESS

The softest thing in the universe,
Overcomes the hardest thing in the universe.

Lao Tzu

Gender abolitionists want to end gender, to destroy gender altogether. They see gender as a supreme organizing principle of society, a principle that must be undone. They want to end the system of birth assignment based on sex, the whole set of expectations associated with that assignment, the coded stereotypes, the patriarchy—the whole thing, gone, destroyed, done away with.

Gender abolitionists imagine a world where men are not assumed to be aggressive in contrast to the meekness and docility of feminine stereotypes, a world where the ideal scientist in people's minds could just as well be a woman or a man. Abolitionists imagine a world where men are not the paradigm of rationality. Other entrapments surrounding gender involving clothing and demeanor are totally neutralized in this gender utopia.

In a nutshell, gender abolitionists seek to equalize and/or totally demolish the Mars/Venus stereotypes surrounding the gender system, the cultural institution of agreeing "women are like this" and "men are like this." In this world, it would be totally normal for women to be aggressive and men to be emotional, for women to be war-like and domineering and men to be submissive, for women to be genius entrepreneurs and men to be experts in domesticity and child care.

In this version of abolitionism, all the "go-getter," male, chief executive stereotypes such as aggression, dominance, taking up space, would be equally distributed in the population. For the abolitionist, all gender stereotypes are bad—without justification—and so in the ideal world there would be no basis on which to form the stereotypes because the underlying asymmetry behind them would no longer exist.

But this is not a world I want to live in. I do not want a mosaic of gendered behavior, a random grab bag of stereotypically male and female traits. In my gender utopia, all the "soft" characteristics associated with femininity in terms of communication style would be held by *everyone*. That is, the ideal distribution of aggressive and docile traits would eliminate the aggression entirely and replace it with the softness stereotypical of women.

We have given male leadership a try—for thousands of years—and it doesn't seem to be working. Can you imagine a global political leadership summit where all major decisions were made by women and/or men who had the same communication style stereotypically associated with women? What kind of world would we live in if men were more incentivized to do the emotional labor so common for women/femmes?

But what is this stereotype of feminine communication, exactly? I think it's most helpful to think about what it's not: it's not constantly interrupting. It's not aggressive. It's not combative. It's not taking up too much space in the conversation. It's not full of bravado. It's not warlike. This style of communication is about active listening, focusing on what the other person saying and not what your response is going to be. It's putting yourself in the other person's shoes. It's more focused on support and validation rather than problem solving or one-upmanship. It's softer in every respect.

Above all it's about vulnerability. As Brene Brown[5] famously argued, vulnerability is a sign of strength, not weakness. It is the shared vulnerability that women have with each other that allows them to open up and deal with the real issues at hand, cutting to the core of the tension and developing a space to foster problem solving.

While men are typically associated with *practical* problem solving because of their "rationality," women are commonly accused of bringing emotions into the mix and ruining every-thing. But I think this stereotype should be reversed: the *lack* of emotional vulnerabiltiy in male problem solving leads to myopia and hubris, with men bulldozing their way through a problem and leaving a trail of abused people in their path. The "straight shooter," "tell it' like I see it," "brutal honesty" style associated with male communication has hidden collateral damage that is often absorbed by countless unthanked women.

So in my gender utopia, softness would be recognized as being the strongest and most practical communication style because it recognizes the long-term, "practical" benefit of emotional labor. Everything else would just be considered reckless and inhumane, and strongly discouraged. We should expect the same of all children in terms of how they communicate with others.

My hypothesis is that the softness of femininity is in all respects a superior communication strategy for human society when compared with the hardness of masculinity. Obviously, a total populational shift in such communication dynamics has never been achieved before. But I am willing to bet that local and global politics, office and workplace dynamics, domestic life, and romantic relationships would be transformed for the better.

I do not have any evidence to substantiate this hypothesis. I'm not a scientist. My goal is merely to open our minds towards the conceptual possibility of a total shift in gender dynamics, a shift towards softness. The mere thought of such a gender utopia is radical in so far as it counters the typical narrative of "balance" between Mars and Venus. But we don't need balance. We need a fresh start. We have had thousands of years of trying to find balance within the current structures of the Mars/Venus dichotomy. Although much progress has been made, the culture of toxic masculinity is still alive and well and continues to actively harm people of all genders.

In the end, the gender abolitionists offer us a solution that does not work to abolish gender so much as sweeps the problem under the rug through the illusion of equality and "balance." Evening up the balance of hardness and softness in the population will do nothing to counter the unhealthy power imbalance at the heart of the Mars/Venus dynamic. In order to truly leap forward, we need to enact a radically experimental attitude that is willing to truly embrace the superiority of softness.

13

NOBODY IS TRANS ENOUGH

Labeling someone a man or a woman is a social decision.

Anne Fausto-Sterling, Sexing the Body

A famous psychology study once took a classroom of kids and randomly divided them into two teams: "red shirts" and "blue shirts." After about a week, the researchers asked the children their opinions about the "other" team. Answers given back were akin to "Those red shirts are dumb and nasty." In other words, the children had taken a purely arbitrary cultural marker—shirt color—and used that as the basis of an elaborate system of discrimination and stereotyping. The takeaway is that children have a natural predilection for "isms"—racism, sexism, ageism, classism—on the basis of cultural markers.

Another takeaway is the natural human tendency to form hierarchies of power. The red shirts saw themselves as superior to the blue shirts, who were clearly an inferior sub-class of human. We see this natural tendency to punch down everywhere. Religious people often form spiritual hierarchies of who's more "pure" than others. Sports fans believe they are superior to other fans. Nerd fandoms form hierarchies of who the "real" nerds are. Academics form hierarchies of power based on perceived "genius." Gamers form hierarchies of who are "serious" gamers vs "casual" gamers.

The examples can be multiplied. The point is that within every cultural domain humans have a tendency to be in a group where everyone should, in theory, be natural allies but then divide themselves over some arbitrary bullshit in order to make themselves feel superior.

LGBT+ people do this too. Bisexual people are routinely discriminated against by gay men and lesbians as being less valid in their LGBT+ identity.

Trans people are especially bad at this. Binary trans people often see themselves as "more trans" than, say, a non-binary trans person who was assigned female at birth (AFAB) but still presents a feminine gender expression. These latter trans people are often accused of being "fakers." They are "transtrenders." Their trans identity is the result of social contagion, not Gender Dysphoria™.

Furthermore, early transitioners often think of themselves as "more trans" than someone who didn't figure it out until their 60s. Those who pass are seen as more valid in their gender than those who do not. Those who conform to binary gender stereotypes are often seen as superior. Those with certain types of childhood experiences or certain kinds of dysphoria are seen as "more trans" than people with different experiences. Usually, the more intense the dysphoria about the body, the "more trans" people are assumed to be.

The point is that trans people shit on other trans people about who is "trans enough." This also leads to individual trans people wondering if they themselves are "trans enough." This process of self-doubt leads to repression of the desire to transition and leaves latent gender dysphoria untreated for years, decades even.

But in reality, *nobody* is trans enough because we can as individuals never fully embody some arbitrary stereotype of what it means to be trans. We can never live up to these standards because the criteria are arbitrary and constantly shifting.

What about gender non-conforming people? Like cross-dressers? Or drag queens? My view is that if these people *don't* disavow their assigned-at-birth gender, if they *don't* take the trans label on themselves, then we shouldn't foist it on them. But if in good faith a gender non-conforming person calls themselves trans but says they have minimal to no bodily dysphoria, who am I to say they are not trans?

Do I, a medically transitioning dysphoric trans girl, have anything in common with a gender non-conforming, non-dysphoric, assigned male at birth (AMAB) crossdresser? It depends. Will they go on to later transition? Do they deep down want to and they're just repressing it? Who knows? I can't see into the recesses of their mind and determine their True Trans Identity. Because after all, most trans people would agree that when someone comes out as trans they don't *start* being trans that moment—they have always been trans but just didn't know it. And since I can't know for sure if a gender non-conforming person will or will not later go on to adopt a trans identity, who am I to completely disavow them from the transgender umbrella? After all, I used to wear women's clothing which was technically "crossdressing" but I later came out to myself—who's to say the gender non-conforming crossdresser won't also do the same?

Furthermore, I think there is political power in making the umbrella as large as possible. The more voices are walking under the trans flag, the more power we have in the system. Making ourselves heard is a key step in advancing our rights, and banding together under a common political framework is useful for building progressive movements. The women's movement has shown that intersectional approaches—acknowledging our different intersecting dimensions of class, race, gender, and so on—have tremendous latent potential for bringing about social change.

14

THE THREE WAVES OF TRANS FEMINISM

Anyone familiar with the history of feminism knows people often talk about "waves." Although the finer details are debated, we can largely break the history of feminism into three waves.

The first wave of feminism was the suffragettes, the women who fought for their right to vote and their inclusion in civil society.

The second wave of feminism was exemplified by *The Feminine Mystique* by Betty Friedan,[6] and represents a move to achieve parity and equality with men, to end sexism in domestic life, to give more economic opportunities to women, and basically bring women out of the kitchen and into society as equals.

The third wave of feminism is largely a response to the inadequacies of the second wave, which mostly centered on the voices of well-to-do white women. The third wave has been referred to as the rise of "intersectional feminism," which looks not just at gender discrimination but how that intersects with race, socio-economic background, disability, gender identity, and so much more. In a nutshell, the third wave represents an attempt to bring to life the saying "the personal is political."

Just like feminism itself, the history of trans activism can be broken down into three large waves. Granted, this reading of trans history is based on my own perception of what's important, but I think my observations are true to the broad trends of the movement.

The first wave of trans feminism

The first wave of trans feminism is exemplified by Christine Jorgensen. Jorgensen, born in 1926, was highly influenced by Paul de Kruif's book *The Male Hormone*,[7] through which she surmised that hormones were the key to her lifelong struggle with gender.

Jorgensen had gone to a pharmacy and asked for estradiol tablets, saying she was a medical technology student studying hormonal growth in animals. "How strange it seemed to me that the whole answer might lie in the particular combination of atoms contained in those tiny, aspirin-like pills."[8]

Jorgensen traveled to Denmark, and once in Europe she finally met with endocrinologist Dr. Christian Hamburger, who oversaw her sex change free of charge with the promise of complete cooperation. Hamburger administered estrogenic hormones and monitored her levels through daily urine samples. Under Hamburger's guidance, Jorgensen received hormone treatments for two years.

In Jorgensen's letter to her family coming out as transsexual (though she did not use this term) she famously said, "Nature has made a mistake, which I have corrected, and I am now your daughter."[9]

In the early 1950s, Jorgensen returned to the States and the *New York Daily News* ran a front-page story "Ex-Gi Becomes Blonde Beauty." The story quickly became a worldwide media sensation and Jorgensen was launched into international fame, a position of notoriety that she struggled with for the rest of her life. Jorgensen became famous but much of the attention came in the form of jokes at her expense. She spent the rest of her life performing a variety show in small clubs and doing speaking events across the country.

Jorgensen exemplifies the first wave of trans feminism for several reasons:

- She was a rare specimen, a singular, shining example of being different.

- The media focus was on the details of surgery and the novelty of transition itself.

- She was a pioneer in almost every way, from hormone treatment to surgery, to the path of transition itself.

The second wave of trans feminism

The second wave of trans feminism is best exemplified by its peak, which in my mind was Laverne Cox's appearance on the cover of *Time* magazine with the headline "The Transgender Tipping Point." This wave represents trans people coming out of the shadows, becoming normal members of society, finding normal jobs and living boring, mundane lives. The second wave was akin to the second wave of feminism itself, representing a push to end discrimination in housing, employment, healthcare, and so on.

Arguably, we are still partially in this wave as trans people are still struggling for acceptance as normal members of society. But it would be naive to think we haven't made great progress.

Philosophically, the second wave of trans feminism was exemplified by Sandy Stone's response in the 1990s to Janice Raymond's famous hit-piece with her article "The Empire Strikes Back: A Posttranssexual Manifesto."[10] This article, more than almost anything else, brought trans studies to the mainstream, introducing post-humanist trans ideas into mainstream feminist theory. The article was central to the development of the burgeoning field of trans studies.

The second wave of trans feminism was still largely couched in the framework of "transsexuals"—trans people who seek medical/surgical solutions to their gender issues. This was the framework for the entire trans movement starting with the first wave: it sought to make the condition of being trans a medical issue distinct from transvestism (gender non-conformity), and the issue was to be solved with the help of medical authorities. And because of this, trans people needed to assimilate into society as good, respectable people, not upsetting the boat too much.

Moreover, the second wave was largely binary in nature—trans people identified strongly as either men or women. In the 1990s we started to see people begin to fight against this "respectability politics" starting with Kate Bornstein and her genderqueer antics. Which brings me to the third wave.

The third wave of trans feminism: the future is fluid

The third wave of trans feminism is all about fighting the gender binary. It's about non-binary identities, gender fluidity, genderqueer, genderfucks, androgyny, gender non-conformity, alternate pronouns, and so on.

Before I go on, I want to reiterate that I am trying to act as a neutral historian in this essay. I am *not* imposing any morality here. My official stance on the third wave is that of neutrality. I know a lot of people, including many trans people themselves, view the non-binary movement with skepticism and disdain. It has become the butt of jokes, indicative of the larger "social justice warrior" movement and the "snowflake liberals." They see this development as largely a bad thing.

I view it as neither good nor bad. It is simply the evolution of modern queer culture. It's a fact. It's happening. I see it happening all around me. As I see it, we have three options. We can: (1) Fight it (2) Promote it or (3) Be neutral.

My official position as historian and observer of trans culture is that of neutrality. I have some theoretical questions about this movement, but I do not want to stand in the way of history happening, especially when so many people feel their personal identity is at stake. And this is where things are moving, so why fight it?

If you look on the non-binary wiki (https://nonbinary. wiki/wiki/Nonbinary), some of the common identities used by people in this movement include (this list is taken directly from the wiki):

- Agender, also known as genderless, non-gender—having no gender identity or no gender to express (similar to and sometimes used interchangeably with gender neutral and/or neutrois).

- Androgyne, also known as androgynous gender—identifying or presenting between the binary options of man and woman or masculine and feminine (similar to and sometimes used interchangeably with intergender).

- Multigender (may also include androgyne)—moving between two or more different gender identities at different times/in different situations or having more than one gender identity at one time. Some multigender identities are bigender, polygender, and genderfluid.

- Gender neutral, also known as neutral gender—having a neutral gender identity and/or expression, or identifying with the preference for gender neutral language and pronouns.

- Genderqueer, also known as genderqueer—non-normative gender identity or expression. While genderqueer originated as an inclusive umbrella term, it is also considered by many to be an individual identity.

- Intergender—having a gender identity or expression that falls between the two binary options of man and woman or masculine and feminine.

- Neutrois—belonging to a non-gendered or neutral gendered class, usually but not always used to indicate the desire to hide or remove gender cues.

- Nonbinary or non-binary—identifying with the umbrella term covering all people with gender outside the binary, without defining oneself more specifically. Is also used as an individual identity in itself. One could be non-binary butch or non-binary femme.

- Transgender—identifying with the umbrella term covering all gender identities or expressions that transgress or transcend (go beyond the limits of) society's rules and concepts of gender. (Transgender is a wide umbrella term also covering people who hold binary gender identities and expressions but who transgress gender by transitioning between the binary genders.)

If your first response to this list is "That's ridiculous!" then you are on the "fight it" side of things. If your response is "Yes! This makes perfect sense!" then you are on the "promote it" side. If your response is, "That's interesting—I need to think about this more" then you are on the "neutral" side. Personally, I am somewhere in-between promote it and neutrality. And part of my promotion is merely the logical conclusion of neutrality: this is where things are heading and I don't want to be on the wrong side of history.

Furthermore, as someone who has dated a non-binary person and knows many strongly identified non-binary people, I know they are genuine and heartfelt in their identities. This is not going to change because someone called them a snowflake.

We can debate all day about whether they are "really trans." But what does it even mean to be "really trans?" Is there an immutable eternal referent for that term? Language changes and evolves. Culture evolves. LGBT culture is certainly not immune to change and evolution. Things might seem to happening awfully fast but I think that's just a function of social media. Kate Bornstein was popularizing her genderqueer identity back in the 1990s, and the history goes back even further.

Furthermore, one could make the argument that non-binary identities have existed in non-Western cultures for thousands of years before the Christian West imposed the gender binary on these cultures by force via colonization. So there is a worldwide tradition of identifying outside the gender binary without relying on hormones and surgery—we in the West are usually just ignorant of this history.

Conclusion

We are still living the second wave of trans feminism, but the third wave is picking up steam. It will have monumental impacts on public discourse and how we organize public space: will the binary public restroom system be viable going forward for the next few hundred years? How much do you have to "look like a woman" to be allowed in "women only spaces?" Do we as a society still need such spaces? This issue is bound to continue causing controversy. This is not going away. It is going to be a political issue for the foreseeable future. Be prepared for tensions to be raised high, for ideology and propaganda to spread virulently on both sides of the debate. A lot is at stake. This is important. We would be naive to simply ignore what's happening. But I hope this reading of history is helpful for providing some context.

LIFE IN TRANSITION

15

LET US GROW

Trans women are under intense pressure, internal and external, to perform femininity to a high level. They are seen as more "valid" in their identities the better they pass for cis women, and in order to compensate for testosterone poisoning some trans women are pressured to wear makeup, accessories, and feminine styles of clothes to be gendered properly by strangers as well as to fight their dysphoria. The common assumption is that trans women who are uber feminine are just narrow-minded 1950s housewife artificialities who are putting on a costume to validate their own womanhood.

Our femininity is never seen as natural, always artificial.

But in reality, it's often about pure survival, a defense mechanism. If we don't perform femininity at a high level, we get accused of being too manly and our womanhood is challenged and we are at more risk of misgendering, harassment, violence, and being discriminated against in general. But if we are feminine, we get shit for just being caricatures of womanhood who think being a woman is all about dresses and heels. It's a double-bind: damned if you do, damned if you don't—trans women lose either way.

But I don't think the problem here is about femininity. The problem is that people don't like the idea of a male-assigned person transitioning socially and medically. It's the very idea of trans women that gives people a problem regardless of how well we perform femininity. The double-bind is thus a product of trans misogyny and not fundamental to femininity itself. The problem is that cis identities are seen as fundamentally more healthy and normal than trans identities. And I mean "normal" as in "normative" not "statistical." Trans people are obviously in the statistical minority, but that alone doesn't make our bodies or our identities pathological—anomalous but not necessarily pathological. Trans women often get a lesser metaphysical status in the realm of valid identities but there's nothing about our transness that is itself intrinsically pathological.

As philosophers like to say, you can't derive an "ought" from an "is." It is the case that trans people are rare, but from that it doesn't entail that we ought to eradicate trans identities. Imagine if we found a "trans gene" that caused transness and scientists had the power to edit that out before or after conception. We as a society would then have a choice whether to eradicate transness out of existence or not. My view is that the world would be much worse off if trans people weren't around to shake up the cis-normative world.

Part of the pressure on trans women to perform femininity comes from a desire to relieve dysphoria. If I lived on a deserted island that had a Sephora, I would still wear makeup because I just enjoy it and it makes me feel better about myself. But part of the pressure comes from how trans women are judged as less valid if we are not uber feminine.

But here's the thing: trans women are often not even given a chance to grow into their femininity. As soon as we come out as trans we are expected to perform femininity flawlessly. We are expected to know how to do makeup, how to be stylish, have an extensive wardrobe of gender-affirming clothing, look sharp, natural, and so on. But cis women have had decades to learn how to perform femininity, experiment with makeup, style, and figure out what looks good for their body shape. Not to mention, not all trans women can afford laser or electrolysis, and the makeup techniques to flawlessly cover beard shadow are pretty advanced even for experienced makeup junkies.

Some trans women have been performing femininity from a very young age but that's not true of all of them. Some trans women such as myself repressed their feelings deeply and went through very "macho" stages to prove their masculinity to the world before their feelings finally surfaced fully and it was no longer possible to perform masculinity without great pain. But the little crossdressing I had done in secret since childhood did not even slightly prepare me for the pressure to perform femininity as a transitioned woman. The pressure is felt by all women but trans women feel it especially acutely. I basically had to learn in a couple years what it took decades for cis women to figure out.

However, some trans women are just not interested in all that and they should not be judged for it, no more than cis women should be judged for being butch or tomboys. The "tomboy" trans woman is often judged as less valid than feminine trans women. Many cis women say they are not scared of highly feminine cis passing trans women who have medically transitioned—it's all those other, "bad ones" they are scared of in women-only spaces, the ones who don't perform femininity to some arbitrarily set cis-normative standard.

We need to let trans women grow into themselves. We are expected to perform femininity flawlessly within months of transition but often it can take years to come into a natural sense of style just like it takes years for cis people to figure out how to perform their genders. We need to let trans women have the space and time to explore themselves before we judge them as "successful." Or better yet, how about we stop judging people who don't conform to any gendered expectation and stop placing judgments on whether a transition is a "success" or not?

If the trans person is happy at the end of the process it was a success, period. TERFs like to talk about how many trans women are just "pigs in wigs" but usually they are just selectively sampling from trans women just starting to transition. Give them a few more years and get back to me. Let trans women grow. Give us time to figure this shit out without invalidating our identities because we have the audacity to look or sound like ourselves and not just flawless imitations of cis women.

Trans people are valid regardless of whether people have a hard time telling whether we are cis. That shouldn't be the standard. There are no standards. Find me a rule book in the universe that tells me how men and women ought to look. There is no such book. There are just atoms in the void—but we place value on some arrangements of atoms and not on others. All value is created from the minds of creatures such as ourselves. Cis people often don't place much value on trans lives. Our lives are seen as diseased.

Just the other day someone commented on my YouTube channel saying that I am "sick" and "need help." Yeah, that's a fun notification to get on my phone. That's just part of what it's like to be trans in 2018. And I have it easy! I am very, very privileged as a trans woman, both in terms of passing and my material status, but I still get constant reminders that my existence is seen by many in this country as an existential threat to the moral fabric of society. Here I am just trying to survive and somehow I am the threat to society? Yeah, right.

Let trans women grow. Not all trans women have had a strong sense of identity since childhood. That's the narrative that plays well with cis audiences, and trans women are under immense pressure to reshape their histories to conform to that narrative but it's not representative of the diversity in the community. Some of us need time to unlearn old patterns of behavior and learn new patterns. Some of us need time to figure out simple things that cis women take for granted, like putting your hair up in a bun.

Many of us were not taught by female members of our family how to perform femininity. If anything, we were usually punished for displaying the slightest amount of femininity. So how can cis people turn around and expect trans women to be perfect exemplars of femininity when at the same time they stamp out femininity in their own male-assigned children? It's the double-bind of trans femininity.

When you start to look, the double-bind is everywhere. We cannot escape it. But we must. The liberation of trans women cannot happen unless the double-bind is loosened and we are allowed to grow.

16

EARLY DAYS OF TRANSITION

A phenomenology of change

When I reflect on my early days of transition I often cringe so hard it feels traumatic. The way I would act, my thought processes, the outfits I would wear...it was...embarrassing. I had no idea what I was doing and had very little guidance except internet research (mostly forums).

Imagine spending your whole life trying to learn how to act as one gender in order to not be punished by society and then doing a 180 and start doing exactly what society has told you not to do.

It was maddening, the thousands of small things that I had to learn and unlearn in the process of transition so as to adjust to my new social reality, and by "reality" I mean the attempt to take my body, ravaged by years of testosterone exposure, and go out in the world and not be beat for up for being a "dude in drag." That was and remains the standard operational goal: don't get read as man.

Luckily, I didn't have to adjust to wild changes in mood as I started hormone replacement therapy (HRT)—so often trans women start the tumultuous process of social change while they are also rewiring their entire hormonal system, switching to a hormone balance that is well known for amplifying the intensity of emotional experience. Couple this with tentative evidence about the most common US-prescribed androgen blocker, spironolactone, increasing susceptibility to stress and you have a combination so common there is a term for it in the trans feminine community: the "rollercoaster."

I remain to this day very stable in my mood. But the learning process was overwhelming at times. Imposter syndrome was in full swing. It's a strange feeling walking around as if you are going to be "found out" at any moment. To this day, my worst fears in this regard have not come true. I have not had a dramatic, "You're not who you say you are!" type situation in public. And that comes from how I have *some* amount of passing privilege (though I do not pass 100 percent and often still get misgendered). But I pass enough if I am trying. And I consider myself lucky in that regard.

One of the primary mechanisms of gendered behavior learning in cis-normative society is attention: who do we pay attention to when we are consciously and unconsciously asking ourselves, "How should I act?" Do we watch the men or the women? The boys or the girls? Who are the "role models" we look to in times of uncertainty? Having spent my life convinced by everyone around me that I was a boy and should act like a boy (punishment, of course, was always looming as a threat against violating these "natural" expectations), I always looked to the masculine people in my life to imitate their behavior. I was fairly good at this and eventually it became internalized, though I was never super macho. I was a scrawny, introverted little kid with a stutter who loved to read and had an active imagination but also loved to be outside and active in the Florida sunshine.

The decision to transition changed the locus of my social attention, with the focus shifting away from men and their associated masculinity. What was internalized for cis women after decades of practice seemed 100 percent natural to them. I had a lot of catching up to do. It's painful to reflect on my memories of the early days of transition where I didn't pass very well and still retained many of my old habits and thought processes. It took months and months to eventually find some sense of myself as a trans woman that was natural and intuitive. Now more than three years on, I am still learning to be myself. Nothing feels as awkward as it once did. I have developed my own sense of style and feel at home in my new body. I like being me.

In reality, there's not a whole lot separating the genders. The performative aspects can be learned in no time if you're a quick study. The part that took longer for me was to internalize the outer performance as part of my personal identity, to truly accept myself as a woman. For many reasons, I still don't quite fully identify as a "woman," whatever that is supposed to mean. I don't have a strong sense of sexual identity and my gender identity is nebulous at best. I just feel like myself, a consciousness staring out behind my eyes, beholding the world.

By now I play the part well enough. As I write this I think about how TERFs would twist my words to argue that "Look! This trans woman admits her femininity is a fabricated artificiality of conscious design!" But my response would be that this is true of everyone, not just me. Although the unconscious does the bulk of learning, consciousness is still involved in very important types of learning and I believe some of the learning is about gender and gender roles. While one might argue that certain innate neural dispositions are genetic, much of human development is learned. The human brain is a fantastically powerful learning machine and it stands to reason that much of our gendered behavior is learned as well and that our consciousness works to direct some part of the learning process.

The thing that makes my learning process different from others is that it's done late in adulthood when my consciousness and brain are already fully developed. In some ways, this gives me an advantage and in some ways, it is a disadvantage. The advantage is that I can largely skip much of the "awkward teen years" of experimentation and get that done in months, not years. As an adult, my learning process is sped up because it's being aided by my full sense of consciousness. The disadvantage is that the "natural" route of learning everything in childhood seems to make it more intuitive because the learning process is so ingrained. Also, children learn about gender more unconsciously whereas I have the advantage of an adult education.

TERFs like to think that the first, say, 10–20 years of our life are our learning destiny, that if we are raised male and socialized as male then we'll always have those "male-like" tendencies that arose from that learning process. But I think this is a dim picture of the powerful capacity of the human brain to change itself. Learning chess changes the brain in deep ways, so surely learning a whole new gender role also changes the brain in deep ways, as does changing the primary sex hormone that your brain runs on. The combination of HRT and gender role change works to reshape the basic way the brain looks at the world.

When I reflect on who I used to be, it seems like a strange dream. I barely recognize myself in certain ways. In other ways, I am the same person, with a "new look." So what is it? New person or not? Has enough of me changed to warrant saying I am a "whole new person?" Philosophers are of no help in giving a decisive answer: it'll depend on who you talk to. Some might say I am the same biological entity as I have been since birth and that grounds my identity so my personhood has never changed. The more "brain-based" theorists might tell me that transition brings about enough significant psychological changes to warrant personhood change.

Some trans people insist that in transition they didn't change their genders, they changed their bodies to align with the gender they've been since birth. But for me, I don't think I really had a well-defined sense of gender at birth. It had to be shaped into existence by the regulations of society on how boys and girls are "supposed" to act.

Don't get me wrong: I am not talking about the "men are from Mars, women are from Venus" type nonsense. I think there are probably more ways in which men and women are alike than they are different. But there are very different power structures at play in the oppression of women and how women are socialized. To downplay the differences and emphasize similarities is not to deny that there are many stark differences between how men and women act. Man-splaining, man-terrupting, taking up space are all examples. As someone who has been in the trenches of a gender transition for over three years and is hyper-vigilant to gendered differences, I can attest to the numerous differences. But many of the differences stem from different learning experiences, not differences in innate "male or female energy" or any bio-social essentialist nonsense that radical fems like to talk about.

I don't believe childhood experience is destiny. The brain can keep on changing for the rest of our lives, sometimes in profound ways. Trans people are testament to that. Biology isn't destiny and experience isn't destiny. Nothing is destiny. We all contain within ourselves the capacity to change greatly. There's been a lot of nonsense spewed lately about how trans women are not "real" women because our childhood experiences were different and we likely received different learning histories growing up. But the thing is, gender happens to be one of those metaphysical categories that is amenable to metamorphosis. And surprisingly, so is sex. The combination of HRT and social transition is remarkably powerful at changing people to their cores. It certainly changed me, for the better I might add.

17

LEARNING TO SAY "FUCK IT" TO PASSING

Like other trans people I am hyper-aware of all gendered subtleties in my vicinity. I am constantly aware of people using pronouns and my brain is constantly performing complex calculations to determine if any particular "he" or "she" refers to me. If I see a man walking down the sidewalk, I usually focus on whether and to what extent his walking style corresponds to the typically exaggerated swagger of men, what I call the "cowboy shuffle."

For probably the first 10–11 months of my transition I put a lot of effort into trying to make my voice more passable. I would spend hours performing various vocal exercises to strengthen the muscles in my voice box necessary to raise my pitch and resonance into the female range. It's a strange feeling opening your mouth and feeling acutely just how "wrong" your own voices sounds. It's highly distressing but since taking an oath of silence is not a viable option I am forced by necessity to either suffer in silence or attempt to adjust my expectations.

My results were not fantastic, probably because I never saw a professional voice therapist. And now I've just given up entirely because I am trying to learn to say "fuck it" to passing. But it's hard. I want to interact with people just for once and not have them question my gender. I would like my gender presentation to be innocuous—an experience I have almost forgotten. But I do remember what it was like pre-transition, to have a mode of expression that was not entirely at odds with the demands of society. While yes, I had long hair for a man and was generally more "metro" than most,[1] I did not stray *too* far from the narrow boxes of expression deemed acceptable for those born with a penis.

I often wonder what it would be like to be *truly* perceived as female, and not just a fleeting impression like someone thinking I'm a woman from across the street. I want just for once to have a one-on-one conversation with someone and not have them suspect I was born male. Although I do honestly feel as if many cis women have included me in the Inner Circle of Womanhood, I sometimes wonder about the epistemic chasm of simply not knowing what it's like to be a cis woman among cis women.[2] Are there things they talk about that they wouldn't talk about in front of a trans woman? It's not that I distrust my cis female friends, it's that I will simply never know what I can't know and must learn to live with that uncertainty.

I suppose I am lucky though. I fall into that strange class of trans women who don't pass perfectly as cis women but people nevertheless (sometimes) say are attractive. The very concept of a beautiful non-passing trans woman is almost a contradiction in terms. If you don't pass, you necessarily look more "mannish" than a cis woman—yet how can a woman who looks like a man be considered beautiful? And yet it's definitely a thing—I myself find many trans people beautiful even if I can "tell" (a locution which itself raises so many questions about the double-bind of authenticity trans people face on a daily basis). Beauty and passing are not the same. You can pass but not be beautiful. And you can be beautiful but not pass.

So I guess I don't have it that bad. I've been accused by others in the local trans community of being the "epitome" of passing privilege, which feels ridiculous given how regularly I am misgendered. I guess the grass is always greener.

But I live my own experience and I know from how I interact with strangers that I get clocked pretty much every time because of my voice. So I don't actually have passing privilege because I don't pass as a cis woman—I am "clockable" as we say.

I often suspect I get read as an extremely feminine man. It is currently impossible for me to go stealth. Most people are polite or smart enough to not "sir" me but I don't always get those gendered pronouns I so crave for validation. My experiences are often genderless despite me observing other people nearby getting gendered correctly. I'll be in a line at the store and the person at the register is gendering everyone in line either male or female, but when they get to me they will refrain from using a pronoun or honorific. I pass enough to largely be avoided being gendered male[3] but not enough to be consistently gendered female, especially after I open my mouth. At the intercom for a drive-through? Forget about it. Over the phone? This one is hit or miss. On older landlines, I notice I get gendered female more often compared with on my cellphone. It also depends on whether I am performing my "customer service voice," which is excessively high-pitched and dripping with feminine up-swing.

So, is there is a secret to learning how to say "fuck it" to passing? No. I have no universal advice. For some people, it's literally impossible to totally say "fuck it" to passing. Their dysphoria is too high for that. I've been blessed to have relatively low levels of dysphoria. Others are not so lucky and they literally cannot ignore the pressing concerns of passing. For some, passing is an omnipresent concern. The state of their bodies in so many small, particular ways is a source of anxiety. The mirror is a place of despair but also occasional glimpses of salvation. For many, it is avoided altogether (an ex of mine had at one point a sheet over the wall-length mirror in her bathroom). Rumination can be intense and hellish, often leading to suicidal thoughts.

I will not attempt to give actionable advice for these people struggling with dysphoria so badly—I've seen from first-hand experience that words of validation do not penetrate to the inner halls of self-worth. All I can offer is the full extent of my empathy and a hug (if wanted).

My advice, instead, is for the people who have the privilege of being able to learn to say "fuck it" to passing. If you have that internal freedom in autobiographical narrative, it's possible to learn to care less about passing. And if you live in an area of the world that is relatively friendly to trans people, or at least not actively unfriendly, then you too can learn to say "fuck it" to passing. Otherwise, passing remains for many across the world a matter of life and death, not an exercise in self-understanding.

The number one goal is to learn to not care what others think of you. Easier said than done. Strive to have the spirit of Kate Bornstein inside you:

> From the moment I learned the word fuck when I was ten years old, I've lived my life with What the fuck am I? Where the fuck do I belong? Who's ever gonna call me family, knowing who and what I really am? Paradox? Bring it on.[4]

It is possible to foster this attitude within yourself through deliberate cognitive practice. Say to yourself, "I don't give a shit. Fuck you." It helps. Or at least it helps me. If someone misgenders me, I try to just tell myself it doesn't matter what strangers think of me. What matters is how I am gendered by my friends and people who know me and are close to me. If they see me as a woman, then that's what matters because they actually know me as a person and respect my gender in its true authenticity.

Strangers are just judging you based on surface-level stereotypes about how people are "supposed" to look or sound. Trans woman with deep voice? You're fucked. But I'd rather spend time with people who don't assume that a deep voice makes you less of a woman. It is the company of people like that that I cherish. Strangers are just reacting to the contingencies of my body, not the holism of my personality. Gender is not a surface level phenomenon. It goes into the core of my being. Strangers can't see that, nor should I expect them to.

There are two types of transphobes. Those who can be educated to change their minds and those who can't. The latter type of people are always going see me as a man so my strategy in these cases is simply to challenge stereotypes associated with men. In a way, transphobes use misgendering as a political weapon, to upset trans women and get under their skin, provoking anger which can then be used to "prove" they're still male socialized. Taking the high road while still finding room for your own humanity is part of what Julia Serano describes as the double-bind of trans femininity.[5]

Another tactic transphobes use is to call trans women "male to trans" (MtT) instead of "male to female" (MtF) because they don't believe trans women can actually change their sex. Once male always male—but you can "trans yourself."

One of my personal strategies for learning to say "fuck it" to passing is to flip this kind of transphobic logic on its head. If they're always going to see me as a man no matter what I do, then it ultimately doesn't matter if I put more effort into passing. I'm not going to change their minds. They are a lost cause not worth stressing about because if they think highly passable trans women like Janet Mock are really just dudes then there is no hope for me.

And if I am being brutally honest, learning to say "fuck it" is likely to be nothing more than an elaborate defense mechanism against my own internal transphobia, which itself is fueled by my experience of being misgendered as well as exposure to the many people convinced I am delusional. It's a weird feeling to know that, at any given minute, there is probably someone, somewhere, engaged in a passionated "debate" about my identity as a trans person, as if our existence is a juicy intellectual puzzle. Knowing all that "discussion" is out there has undoubtedly changed the inner landscape of my identity, moving me towards the androgynous. In a world less invested in dissecting my womanhood, "fuck it" would not be my motto.

TERF transphobes are supposedly all about shattering the stereotypes associated with what "males" are meant to be like. So go ahead. Think of me as a man—I have long since grown bored with that label. Femme man or femme woman—ultimately these are just labels with no concrete definition.

People are free to define these terms for themselves how they wish. I have given up on getting the world to unite behind what it means to be a man or woman, male or female, trans or cis. Everyone has their own pet theory, their own grand idea of what gender is "really" all about.

Transphobes think they can dehumanize me by saying I only transitioned from a male to a tranny. But echoing Kate Bornstein—I am proud to be trans! It's an identity I welcome and embrace. Not because being trans is without its problems but because being trans is the only way I can genuinely be myself. My trans identity is a source of many difficulties but it's also a source of great happiness through the power of self-determination and self-actualization.

But I recognize I am speaking from a place of privilege. Not all trans people are lucky enough to see their being trans as anything but a nightmare, a horrible biological malady that they wouldn't wish on their worst enemy. How has the cruelty and transphobia of the world twisted something so beautiful into a tragedy? I am a strong believer in Laverne Cox's hashtag #transisbeautiful. It's a powerful message precisely because so many don't believe it's true. They have been convinced that trans is ugly, sinful, diseased, pathological. But it's only those things because we lived in a fucked-up world. In a utopia, there would be room for trans people not just to exist but to flourish.

Think about that. Think about life in a trans utopia. The very possibility of that imaginary world proves that trans is not inherently pathological[6]—it's not an intrinsically horrible experience. In a perfect world, being trans would be like having freckles, just another thing that makes us unique individuals. In a perfect world, passing wouldn't have the all-importance it does now because safety wouldn't be an issue. If trans people could be assured 100 percent that the world did not pose a physical threat because of their existence, I guarantee so many more people would come out of the closet and transition. So many trans people would learn to say "fuck it" to passing because they can finally just be themselves without worrying about all the pressure to pass.

It is the first type of transphobes, the ones who can be educated, that I truly care about. They are the ones who are merely ignorant about trans identities. Their minds can be changed through getting to know us, learning to appreciate the utter normalcy of our lives and also the unique struggles of our existence.

They can learn about gender and how it's different from physiology (and then at an advanced level learn how it interacts with physiology). They can learn about neuroscience and the biological basis of gender. They can learn about pronouns and how important they are. These are the people who can learn to feel bad after they misgender you. They can't help it—occasional slip-ups are expected. But they can learn. They can change. They can learn to see trans people for who we really are.

It is through this process of education and personal association that trans people have any chance of approximating our trans utopia. By holding on to that ideal, we can develop the all-important idea of hope, what Barack Obama so presciently described as an audacious process. Hope leads to optimism and optimism leads to change, even if just internal change. We are ourselves our own best source for mental contentment and satisfaction. By giving ourselves a chance to accept ourselves we can learn to say "fuck it" to passing and just be ourselves.

This is easier said than done (there is my privilege speaking again). But I am a dreamer. I can't help but imagine a better world for trans people. A world where passing is done only for ourselves, not for others. A world where passing is about being true to our internal image of ourselves, not a defense mechanism against transphobia.

I haven't quite learned how to truly say "fuck it" to passing. I still care about passing very deeply and perhaps always will. But I'm learning. I'm learning there is an alternative way of existing, even if it is an existence that is fleeting. But the moments where I can truly say "fuck it" are magical because it is in those moments where I learn to be myself.

18

HYPER-VIGILANCE IN THE GENDER MACHINE

Did that customer just "sir" me? When he said, "Thanks man," would he have said that to a cis female or was that just for me?

Did that person just say "dude" to me in a gender neutral way or not?

Is my co-worker going to use the right pronoun for me at the end of this sentence? Is there any hesitation in their usage of "she" pronouns for me or is it natural and automatic?

Did that customer just include me in their reference to "ladies?" (*internal leap of joy*).

Pronouns are the primary fuel of the gender machine. The gender machine is the whole apparatus of gender, the constant way in which life on Earth is filtered through the lens of whether you are a man, a woman, or something else. The gender machine is omnipresent, though if you aren't paying attention it can seem as if it doesn't exist at all. The gender machine is brutal and impersonal: you are subject to it regardless of whether you want to be or not. The gender machine is deeply metaphorical:

it provides the foundation for our entire understanding of culture, pop culture, songs, movies, and so on.

Before I transitioned, I only had a passing familiarity with the gender machine. I knew it existed, of course, and was obviously a product of it and regulated by it, but I didn't really know it. I never paid it much attention, with occasional exceptions—being read as a male with long hair and ear piercings was sometimes interesting. Getting punished by my parents as a young child for wearing women's clothes certainly made me aware of the gender machine and the rules of what boys are "supposed" to be like. My relationships with women exposed me to the gender machine a little bit. Being a husband made me self-conscious of my role within the gender system. I had read a bit of gender theory here and there but didn't really understand the gender machine on a super personal level. I was like the proverbial fish who lives and breathes water but doesn't have a concept of water because it surrounds them 24/7.

But nothing prepared me for what it's like to be a wrinkle in the gender machine, a nail that sticks out, an anomaly, a person who was first assigned male, raised male, and regulated as male but who eventually pushed back and bucked the system, who self-consciously rejected their position in the gender machine and chose another path, the path towards womanhood.

But violations in the gender machine are highly regulated by misgendering, transphobia, and enforcement of gender conformity. If you don't look and sound "like a woman," then the gender machine will refuse to play along and you will get hurt. You will get "sirred." You will get nasty stares as you walk out of the bathroom. You will be harassed, threatened, or maybe even violently assaulted or killed. The gender machine will attempt to chew you up and spit you out. You will be called "freak" and seen as less than human. You will suffer slurs.

You will be slandered as a pervert. Your sanity will be called into question. The gender machine has it especially in for non-passing trans women and non-binary trans femmes due to the way masculinity and femininity are strongly regulated for those who are assigned male at birth. Any hint of an assigned-male person dabbling in femininity is brutally regulated so much so that trans women repress their desires for decades, or even repress them forever.

Does my adam's apple stick out too much at this angle? I worry about this as I stand at the counter and adjust how I'm standing so the customer won't see it right away. As Imogen Binnie put it in her novel *Nevada*, "That's what it's like to be a trans woman: never being sure who knows you're trans or what that knowledge would even mean to them. Being on unsure, weird social footing."[7] I maximally "prime" my customers with my available gender cues, minimize the cues I want to hide, and slightly adjust the way I'm standing and holding my head to hide my adam's apple. But I know they'll eventually see it. They always do. That or my voice will reveal my history of being exposed to testosterone. What will they think of me? Not, how will they treat me? Most people are nice. But how will they internally think of me? "Oh, there's one of those ugly trannies. Freak." Or worse. My paranoia about this runs deep. It affects my relationships with people I don't know extremely well. Many TERFs these days are hardcore TERFs but keep their opinions to themselves. That's almost worse. The fake smile. The pretend use of pronouns while secretly thinking, "You're a man."

"Hi, what can I get started for you today?" I speak over the intercom in a strained voice, desperately doing all I can to avoid the inevitable "Sir."

Often I don't get it. But sometimes I do. I wonder if I would get misgendered more if we lived in a time when the gender machine regulated gendered communication and encouraged "sirs" and "ma'ams" at all times. Nowadays, thank God, people are more lax on the honorifics. I personally try to never use them unless absolutely necessary. What's the point? They do practically no good and often cause much harm to trans and gender non-conforming people. My voice is the Ur-factor in how I am perceived within the gender machine. It determines everything. Unfortunately, I know my voice is not perfect and still gets read as male by those unsuspecting strangers who might expect something else out of my mouth based on my appearance or dress.

I wake up super early for work to placate the gender machine with makeup. I know many cis women across the world are pressured by the gender machine to wear makeup to work in order to be seen as "professional," "hygienic," or even "competent," but I am pressured into waking up extra early to shower, shave, and put on makeup in order to maximize my available gender cues, minimize the negative ones, and ultimately reduce my chance of getting misgendered, avoiding dysphoria as much as possible. With my voice and my adam's apple and my masculine features, makeup is a defense mechanism for me, a way to reinforce the gender cues I give off. But what I'd give to have the option to just wear a bare face but still be so effortlessly feminine that no one in their right mind would question my status in the gender machine.

Whether I eventually get misgendered or not depends on many factors, mainly to what extent these people are self-conscious regulators in the gender machine—or transphobic assholes. But it's also ignorance. And not paying attention. But still. Regardless, the most common thing that happens is that people don't gender me at all. I get greeted as female all the time but rarely depart as an acknowledged female. When others around me get pronouns, I often get none. Which isn't too bad I guess. Could be worse.

My co-workers, or "partners" as we call them at Starbucks, are my literal life blood. Their acceptance of me as a woman and their automatic usage of "she" pronouns are my primary coping mechanism for dysphoria and misgendering at work. The small little genderings that happen through the day literally sustain me. It means so little to them, yet so much to me.

Life as a non-passing trans woman for me means constant vigilance within the gender machine. "Professional pronoun detector" should be written on my business card. Constant awareness of all things gender defines my worldview.

When I am hanging out with cis males, I can't help but notice their masculinity and define myself as apart from them, down to tiny little mannerisms like the small inflection they put on the end of a word, or how much space they are taking up. When I am around cis females, I can't help but compare myself with them and feel self-conscious about every little feminine detail that comes so naturally to them. Even hanging out with butch lesbians does little to make me feel better because even they are so dripping with womanhood that I can't help but feel "less." Such is life as a quasi-passing, late-transitioning trans woman.

The gender machine is fueled by pronouns, and regulated by conformity. It is all around us. Even in today's post-modern liberal society of increasing LGBT+ diversity awareness, the gender machine is working harder than ever to regulate gender. It might seem like we are now living in a laissez-faire world when it comes to gender, but don't let surface trends fool you. The growing acceptance of trans and gender non-conforming people in society has done absolutely nothing to placate the gender machine. It is still hungry—it still needs to feed. It simply finds a new tactic, a new way of regulating gender, new rules, regulations, associations, connotations, and expectations.

Gender is still all pervasive, as any trans or observant person will tell you. Some gender theorists like to talk about a future, hypothetical society where the gender machine is no more. But that's a thought experiment only. A fantasy. A utopia that will never come to be. All we can do is force the gender machine to evolve in small, hopefully progressive directions. But despite the gender machine's dominance and finality being out of our control, we can as individuals take self-conscious steps towards understanding our place within it and working to make sure everyone feels safe as they can be. Respecting pronouns and reducing the usage of honorifics is a huge part of this and definitely something cis allies can do. Good luck.

GENDER AND POLITICS

19

MONSTER POLITICS

On being an assemblage

My body is a mismatch—it displays both my history of poisoning and the effects of the antidote (which came entirely too late). My brain is an amalgamation of many intersecting contradictions. A swarming, if you will.

I am a monster—if you listen carefully you can hear the process of me pulling myself apart and putting myself back together again.

My self-knowledge is clouded. I resonate deeply with how Deleuze described the self: a wolf-pack, a multitude, a colony:

> It is not a question of representation: don't think for a minute that it has to do with believing oneself a wolf, representing oneself as a wolf. The wolf, the wolves, are intensities, speeds, temperatures, nondecomposable variable distances. A swarming. A wolfing.[1]

Sometimes I will just be sitting there and suddenly I get this foreboding sense of being a refusal, an unregulated biomass. On good days, I am merely a gendernaut exploring the outer reaches of identity. On bad days, I see myself as a gender terrorist, someone intentionally striking fear into those with strong emotional attachments to the traditional Order of Things.

Often it strikes me that I am not a person in the traditional sense—a better description is that I am a becoming, a process, a field, a flow of atoms. I am, to riff on Carl Sagan, monstrous star stuff.

My only stability is my desire for change, my desire to become someone (or perhaps some*thing*) I am not, a desire to evolve, mutate, and self-assemble into a new configuration free from my history of testosterone, my history of everyone assuming *they* know who I ought to be. I refuse to be comforted by the soft glow of identity. My reality is defined by the concrete texture of my body, face, and voice—"feelings" have little to do with it.

I don't want to be a subject—I want to be a force. My brain has devoured itself, recreating itself in a new image. This image has now become mundane in its everydayness. But it is special and personal and meaningful in a way that few things in life are. And that, I think, is one of the few positives of the trans experience: a real chance at feeling what it's like to live authentically, to *choose life* authentically.

Monster politics actively undermines the integrity of the human body but its goal is actually to undermine the integrity of the soul. Monster politics seeks to destabilize the metaphysics of gender. Gender cannot save us—we must escape from it at maximum velocity. But it's like trying to outrun your shadow or trying to find the edge of the universe—as soon as we get to the end it opens up a whole new reality.

Not everyone is a monster and not everyone *wants* to be a monster but every true monster wants to be a monster. Monsters feed off the fear of everyone else not wanting to be a monster. It is the fuel which drives us to be even more hideous.

The hormones flowing inside my body are not produced within my body. If I did not inject estradiol valerate into my thigh on a regular basis, my body would cease to function normally. Sometimes I reflect on how I will have to do this for the rest of my life (assuming no new developments in biotech emerge, which is unlikely) and it gives me an appreciation (and concern) for how the optimal medical functioning of my body is now inextricably linked with the pharmaceutical-medical-industrial complex.

The problem with monsters is that everyone thinks they are ugly. But on the contrary, monsters are beautiful in the same way that a thunderstorm is beautiful—through sheer energy. Monsters inhabit the part of reality that no one else can. We inhabit the liminal spaces, the in-between-ness, the dimensions that exist outside of the comforting confines of the gender binary.

My gender is monstrous. It cannot be reconciled with the old transsexual narrative of being a woman trapped in a man's body. I am a monster trapped in a non-monstrous body, like a contradiction imprisoned inside a stable field of containment. I stick myself with needles filled with bioidentical hormones to break out of the prison cell that is my body. I am experimenting on my body not because I am in the "wrong body" but because I aim to see just how far my body can change.

The traditional explanation of transgenderism[2] is that I am "uncomfortable in my body." My explanation is that my body is not enough for me. It just doesn't cut it. Discomfort is a watered-down way of saying that I am a monster, a hybrid, a field of intersecting biological contradictions. My body cannot be reduced to a single category. My body refuses easy definitions. My body is an act of terrorism. It confuses those who cannot see the body for what it is: a field of potential.

I am a monster. But that does not define me. Monster politics recognizes that monstrosity itself is monstrous, it cannot be contained within easy conceptual organizations. And don't tell me I am not a monster. Don't tell me I am pure and whole. Don't tell me because I won't believe you.

20

IS THE VERY CONCEPT OF "PASSING" PROBLEMATIC?

If you hang out in trans circles long enough you start to realize the controversy surrounding the concept of "passing." First off, what is "passing?" Typically, for a trans woman to "pass" is for strangers to not realize they were assigned male at birth. In other words, for a trans woman to "pass" is for the random passerby to think she's cisgender, not trans. For this reason, some theorists talk about "cis passing" because that's exactly what it is: passing for a cis person when in fact you are not cis.

And therein lies the controversy: why should cis people be the standard through which we define and understand the appearance of trans folks? To say that cis people are the ultimate standard is to buy into the whole concept of cis normativity, which is the idea that cis people's genders are more valid and real than the genders of trans people. Furthermore, the concept of passing implies that we are trying to "pass ourselves off" as something we are not. Thus, to "pass" can imply that we are being deceptive. A trans woman walks into a woman's restroom and "passes"—does this mean she was pretending to be cis to enter the bathroom?

But that's false—trans people are not being deceptive simply by virtue of walking down the street. How could we be deceptive when we are just trying to be ourselves? When I go to the grocery store I am not "pretending" to be cis, and have zero intention of deceiving anybody. This is the dilemma that trans people face when we have to "come out" to people. Cis people often view this in terms of duplicity but that places trans people in a double-bind. Should we be expected to wear a sign on our heads? There is no way to be "non-duplicitous" by just being ourselves. I am not constantly lying with every footstep I take in public. I'm just being myself.

But there's a conundrum here, which is that trans people, including myself, go out of our way to "pass more" or "pass better" in many circumstances. When I go to the drive-through I try to pitch my voice higher than normal in order to get gendered female over the intercom. Does this mean I am "faking it" in order to pass myself off as something I'm not? If you look at forums like Reddit's /r/transpassing, it's very clear that the vast majority of trans people, if not *all* trans people, care about passing to some extent. If they pass already, that's great, they're happy. And if they don't pass, that's a reason for much consternation. The belief that one will never pass can actually be a reason for some trans people deciding to not transition at all.

And there are very good reasons for trans people to care about passing. First and foremost, it's about our safety. If you pass, you are said to be able to "blend into society." If you don't pass, you stick out and are at greater risk for transphobic violence or harassment. This is especially true for trans women. Sex workers who are "found out" to be trans are often at risk of extreme violence from men. To pass as cis is to be safe. To be visibly trans is to be less safe.

So it's quite rational to care about passing from a pragmatic safety perspective, especially if you are on the trans femme spectrum.

Not passing is also the source of much of gender dysphoria. If you're a non-passing trans woman—everyone can tell you're trans by looking at you or talking to you—this can be a source of depression, anxiety, and suicidal thoughts. Why? Well it's simple. First off, if you don't pass you're more likely to get misgendered, which is painful for trans people. Second, if you don't pass then that means people in society are less likely to see you as your true gender. Third, if you don't pass, then your body does not align with your desires with respect to having the characteristics of the "opposite sex," which leads to dysphoria and therefore suffering. *But wait.*

Weren't we just saying before that cis people should not be the standard by which the appearance of trans people should be judged? Why are cis people the standard? Why can't trans people be judged with respect to their own standard? One of the deepest symptoms of transphobia is to think that more you pass, the more valid your gender is and the less you pass, the less valid or real your gender is. When they see a non-passing trans woman transphobic people are likely to think "that's a man" because she does not pass. It requires a great deal of internal, mental work to correctly gender trans people who do not pass because it is ingrained in our minds that men and women are "supposed" to look a certain way. A 6 foot 5 and 300lbs, broad-shouldered trans woman with a deep voice is automatically thought to be "less valid" than a petite, attractive passing trans woman.

And therein lies the problematic nature of the very concept of "passing." The whole concept reduces gender to a certain set of physical traits. If you don't meet some checklist of physical traits that are stereotypically associated with a certain gender, then your own gender is up for question. Why that is problematic should be obvious. The validity of anyone's gender should never be reduced to the question of having certain physical traits. If a trans woman has a deep voice, that does not make her less of a woman. Or at least that's how things should work in an ideal world. But in the actual world, cis people seem to have a problem properly internally gendering someone who does not pass.

Sure, the good ones might gain a mastery of pronouns and be respectful but there's always the lagging issue of what they "really" think—of how they are internally gendering someone. It's quite possible for someone to use she/her pronouns for a trans woman but deep down see her as a man because she doesn't pass perfectly. And if you think this is just a cisgender phenomenon then you are mistaken because trans people can also be deeply transphobic and harbor the same biases against non-passing trans people. I've seen this in the community over and over, especially in the older generation of trans people who had to make it through the gatekeeping system in order to transition, a gatekeeping system that used to deny HRT/surgery to trans people who weren't deemed passable enough or didn't have enough passing potential.

So is the concept of "passing" deeply problematic? Yes and no. Should we do away with the concept altogether? I don't think so. Clearly passing is important to the trans community. Most if not all trans people care deeply about how well they pass to some extent. But on the flip side I think it is our imperative to spread the message that our validity does not depend on how well we pass. We need to also spread the message that non-passing trans people can still be happy, find jobs, be romantically loved, and live successful, fulfilling lives. Passing should not be the gold standard by which we judge someone's success in transition. However, we cannot ignore the fact that passing trans people have it much easier in our society than non-passing trans people. If you watch the cis media, usually the trans people interviewed or recognized are highly passing trans people, which is unrepresentative of the whole trans community (this is especially true for the community of trans women, but less true for the trans male community which often has an easier time passing after years of testosterone). We need to do a better job to normalize non-passing trans people as being "just as trans" as their passing counterparts. A holdover of the "true trans" era of medical gatekeeping is that "true transsexuals" were believed to be more passable than the people who are not "true transsexuals." But the quest to define who is "truly trans" is a fool's game, and not one worth pursuing because you will inevitably exclude people based on arbitrary criteria such as your height or the deepness of your voice.

Passing is important. And I don't think using substitute terms like "blending" is really going to alter the importance of passing to the trans community. But as we've seen, the concept is also deeply problematic in so far as it implies deception and reinforces cis normativity. Many if not most trans people wish they were cis but that's not true of all trans people. Many trans people are happy being trans and wouldn't change it for the world. I kind of fall into the latter camp. It's beyond this essay to explain in detail why I love being trans, but part of it comes from my intrinsic distaste for normality. I like being different and different I am—I am not your average woman. But many trans people crave normality. They just want to be a normal man or woman in this society. And that's fine. There's nothing wrong with that.

But there's also nothing intrinsically wrong with being trans. It's not an intrinsically horrible life, even in you're non-passing. Sure, living in a transphobic society can make being trans horrible—violence, loss of friends, job, family, harassment, discrimination, lack of healthcare, and so on—all these things can make being trans a nightmare. But those things are not intrinsic to being trans—they are a product of the society we live in. If society was lurched forward hundreds of years and trans people became widely accepted, then things would be very different. The suicide rate would surely go down.

There are many horrible aspects of being trans, such as dealing with dysphoria. But in a perfect society, we would be able to use technology to deal with dysphoria such that it would be drastically reduced in most trans people, especially by letting trans kids get access to blockers and start HRT before becoming masculinized/ feminized by puberty. Greater awareness of trans people would give trans kids role models through which to identify and the average age of transition would probably go down, making HRT more effective and reducing the chances of dysphoria.

So no, I don't think the concept of passing is inherently problematic because it's the only way to adequately deal with gender dysphoria. If passing made no sense conceptually, then the concept of gender dysphoria would also be incoherent. But dysphoria is critical to understanding the trans experience and thus passing is critical as well. But we need to realize that passing is not the be-all-and-end-all of our identities. Non-passing trans people deserve respect and deserve to have their genders recognized without emulating the cis body perfectly. Trans people should not measure their intrinsic worth as people by how well they can pass as cisgender. I know plenty of non-passing trans women who are happy being their authentic selves and go about their life like anyone else without too much concern for whether they pass perfectly. These women are role models of how to live successfully in a society that can be cruel and harsh to non-normative people. And furthermore, we need to spread the message in Laverne Cox's hashtasg #transisbeautiful, which is that trans people are beautiful not just when they pass for cis, but rather, they are beautiful by virtue of not passing as cis.

21

THE "TRUSCUM" DEBATE

The LGBT+ community has been arguing about who belongs under the trans umbrella and who doesn't for decades. Do you have to hate your body to be trans? If so, how strong does that hatred have to be? Do you have to want hormones if you're trans? Do you have to have a gender expression "opposite" to that associated with your birth gender? The boundaries of trans identity are hotly debated and trans people themselves are divided on the issue. Cis people are also invested in this debate. I would wager that at any given time, there are at least two cis people dissecting trans identities as a fun intellectual exercise.

The debate can be distilled down to two competing positions: self-described "truscum" (also called trans medicalists) vs what I will call "maximals." Truscum believe that gender dysphoria is necessary for being trans and that being trans is essentially a medical condition defined by dysphoria and the desire for "opposite" sexed bodily characteristics. In other words, truscum believe that being trans, in its essence, has to do with our relationship to our bodies.

The name "truscum" comes from the concept of "true trans"—the idea that we can develop a way of determining who is "truly trans" vs those who are merely "transtrenders," that is, cis people confused into thinking they are trans for whatever sociological or personal reason, perhaps because they want to fit into niche internet communities or what truscum would call the "special snowflake" phenomenon. On this view, young, vulnerable people are turning to trans identity to find meaning in a world they don't quite fit into.

Before I go on further, I need to point out that trans medicalists themselves have self-consciously reappropriated the term "truscum" to describe their position. A more traditional way of talking about this debate is in terms of separating "true transsexuals" from "merely transgender" people where "transgender" means those trans people who don't want to medically transition and "transsexual" means those that have dysphoria strong enough to necessitate medical transition. But "transsexual" is seen by many as an outdated term that comes from the old-school psychiatric community.

With that said, try to read this essay without thinking the term "truscum" is pejorative. As you will see, I believe there is a huge amount of truth in the trans medicalist position so I'm not bashing the belief system, merely using the term I see most often used by self-described trans medicalists. But the mere fact the word "scum" is being thrown around to describe a position in this debate goes to show just how politically charged this issue is, both within the trans community and outside it.

For example, consider the UK's Gender Recognition Act of 2004, which allows trans people to gain legal recognition of their gender. The process involves going before a Gender Recognition Panel and basically "proving" they are trans enough to warrant a legal recognition of their gender. Trans activists have proposed changes to this Act that would allow trans people to self-identify as their gender without going before a panel. Basically, if you sincerely identify as a woman, the UK government would have to legally recognize that identification.

These proposed changes are controversial because they bring to light the question: is self-identification enough? What if you identify as a woman but make no plans to "pass" as a woman? Should you be allowed to go into woman-only spaces like public bathrooms? Trans medicalists would argue that this proposed change to the Gender Recognition Act goes too far in so far as it goes beyond the traditional focus on gender dysphoria and focuses just on self-identification, which may or may not occur along with dysphoria. But essentially, this debate is about who gets to claim they are trans.

In contrast to the trans medicalists, who want to limit the trans umbrella to those who have significant gender dysphoria, "maximals" tend to believe that dysphoria is not necessary for being trans and generally want to expand the trans umbrella to be maximally inclusive. Maximals sometimes go even further and lump androgynes, gender benders, gender non-conforming people, crossdressers, drag kings/queens, and so on into the "trans" category (although this is an oversimplification I will discuss below).

Maximals also don't believe that being trans is necessarily a medical condition or that if you're trans there's something necessarily "wrong" with you, whereas trans medicalism, as the name implies, wants to exclusively frame transness as a medical, (i.e. pathological), condition defined by medically significant dysphoria.

Instead of defining trans people as those people with gender dysphoria, maximals often define being trans as the state of having a gender that is different from the gender/sex you were assigned at birth. This definition is maximally inclusive because it doesn't require dysphoria in the definition. For example, if you are non-binary, for example "agender," you might not have dysphoria about your body but your gender is different from the gender you were assigned at birth.

Let's get some other definitions out of the way. "Gender dysphoria" is generally defined as a disconnect between the sexed body and your self-model of how you want your body to be. For example, if you were assigned male at birth but feel your body should be female instead, then you have gender dysphoria and vice versa for those assigned female at birth. Dysphoria can also occur for non-binary people who can feel dysphoria about their sexed body.

So what's the beef between these two viewpoints? Trans medicalists often argue they are trying to help "real" trans people get better access to medical care for transition. They also argue they are trying to break down gender stereotypes in so far as they argue that if you're a guy who enjoys femme clothing and makeup, that doesn't necessarily make you trans, and vice versa for butch women. The idea is that crossdressing and gender non-conformity are not enough to be trans—you must be deeply dissatisfied with your sexed body and desire the "opposite" sexed body, otherwise we lose the very distinction between gender non-conforming cis people and trans people.

In contrast, maximals generally argue that the line between gender non-conformity and being trans is fuzzy and hard to pin down precisely. They deny that dysphoria is necessary because they want to deny that gender can be reduced to any physical characteristics such that if you have an assigned-male body you don't necessarily need to medically transition in order to feel comfortable in a female gender identity or live your life socially as a female—and they would go further and argue that society should accept these people as "real" women, just as real as any other woman, cis or trans.

Furthermore, maximals often emphasize that sometimes trans people transition not because they experience gender dysphoria but rather because they experience gender *euphoria*. Gender euphoria is the joy one experiences in taking on a new gender identity, expression, pronouns, social existence, and so on. Euphoria can also be achieved through medical transition. You might not necessarily hate your body but nevertheless desire to medically transition because you believe that would bring greater satisfaction into your life.

Another argument available to maximals depends on transgenderism in non-Western societies. Take native "Two Spirit" people, which is generally the term for trans/gender expansive people in Native American society. The argument goes that being Two Spirit cannot be so easily mapped onto Western ideas of transgenderism which typically revolve around gender dysphoria and medical transition. Instead, transgenderism in non-Western societies or historical contexts generally depends on a more complicated gender role system that is outside the Western male–female binary. But we must be careful because historical trans people sometimes did take steps to alter their bodies; for example, eunuchs in the Bible would sometimes self-castrate. So we can't necessarily say that non-Western transgenderism is entirely divorced from gender dysphoria.

And I will admit frankly I don't know enough about these other cultures to definitely state anything about whether trans people in these societies felt what is now called gender dysphoria. But the general point maximals make is that transgenderism had been around a long time before it was "medicalized" by the West into a pathological condition that needs to be corrected with HRT and surgery. For example, Two Spirit people would not necessarily believe there is anything wrong with being Two Spirit in the sense of it being a medical pathology.

But we need to be careful, as there are some Two Spirit people who do say they have dysphoria and are on HRT to correct it, so Two Spirit tradition and modern medical transition are not at odds necessarily. But we should also be careful to not project the Western framework onto non-Western traditions as a default—if a Two Spirit person wants to use the language of dysphoria, that is their decision, but we should not foist it on them without explicit information given on a case-by-case basis.

But the general point maximals make is that transgenderism in non-Western societies cannot just be reduced to Western conceptions of what it means to be trans because that would be trying to force a complex system of beliefs and social roles into something they're not.

Another argument the maximals can make is to refer to the complexities of how the drag world relates to the world of trans people. Most drag queens are just cis males who enjoy expressing a feminine self from time to time but ultimately don't desire female bodily characteristics and like being able to come home, take off the drag and get back into guy mode.

But if you know anything about drag, you know that some drag queens eventually do go on to identify as trans and to medically transition. These drag queens often continue to perform as drag queens during their transition. Is that fair? Allowing trans women to compete in what is traditionally a male activity? The issue is complicated because gender is complicated and messy, with boundaries between different identities being fuzzy. This is what fuels maximalist arguments: gender non-conformity is an expansive phenomenon that reflects many complex facets of identity and social roles.

However, gender non-conformity in and of itself is not sufficient for being trans. A man who wears makeup is not necessarily trans just because it's non-conformist for men/boys to wear makeup. Similarly, a woman with short hair who shops in the men's section is not automatically trans otherwise we wouldn't have a distinction between butch women and real trans guys. To think otherwise is to buy into sexist stereotypes that men must behave in a certain way in order to be "real men," and vice versa for women. Having interests in cars or Barbies does not define gender. Whether you are assigned male or female at birth cannot predict the range of interests and activities that someone is going to take up in their lifetime. Some men are femme and some women are masc and some people are very fluid in their gender expression.

So who's "right," truscum or maximals? In my view, that debate boils down to a false dichotomy and oversimplification. I take a non-reductionist view of transgenderism. It cannot be defined in terms of necessary and sufficient conditions universal to all trans people, nor can it be reduced to any one physical condition, medical pathology, process of identification, and so on. Where maximals go wrong is in saying that gender dysphoria has nothing to do with being trans. Gender dysphoria is experienced by almost all trans people in some fashion or another, but trans medicalists go wrong in assuming this dysphoria can be defined neatly in terms of desires for the "opposite" sexed body.

First of all, this relies on what Julia Serano[3] calls "oppositional sexism"—the idea that men and women are total opposites. Serano argues that people overlook the massive similarity and overlap between the two sexes and she further argues that the very idea there are only two sexes/genders is overly simplistic when we consider intersex phenomena and complex multi-gender systems in non-Western cultures where there are sometimes upwards of five different genders.

One thing philosophers learn is that there is often a grain of truth to all theories that have been developed by smart people.

There are smart, informed people on both sides of the truscum debate. Both sides think they are doing something to help trans people achieve greater acceptance in society—trans medicalists say they are bringing awareness to medical access for trans people, whereas maximals say they are doing the same thing by focusing on the dangers of trying to give care only to well-defined "true" trans people instead of relying on self-identification. But the problem with the "debate" is that it tries to reduce the phenomenon of transgenderism into a narrow box. Both truscum and maximality are narrow-minded in so far as they try to reduce the complexity of gender and sex to a single ideological system.

In reality, gender is far too complicated for black and white, easy answers. We have to live with the uncertainty of not knowing *exactly* who is and isn't allowed in the women's bathroom. In my view though, rather than trying to define things so precisely to fit into a binary world, we should design the world to accommodate a diversity of genders and gender expressions.

Instead of spending so much energy on trying to decide if the trans woman with a beard is "really" a trans woman or just a crossdressing man, couldn't we just push for unisex public bathrooms? There are plenty of super butch cis women who get frequently misgendered for being "too masculine" and they also run the risk of being falsely kicked out of the women's bathroom when we become so focused on policing gendered spaces. The lesson generalizes: there will always be collateral damage in our fight for clean, well-defined boundaries when it comes to gender.

I think this is just one of those areas in life that will always be messy and probably best sorted out on an individual basis using our good judgment and common sense. We can worry about people taking advantage of the system but there is no way to legislate against people being assholes. We just have to stay vigilant. But that would be true regardless of whether we had a solution to the truscum debate. My answer here might sound like a cop-out but I am only trying to be realistic. There will always be edge cases that challenge our sense of having it all figured out. Instead of worrying about sorting seven billion people into two classes (trans vs cis), can we just try to get along as reasonable adults operating with common sense?

22

RADICAL FEMINISM, ESSENTIALISM, AND NORMALITY

Gender critical radical feminists ("GCers") believe that trans women are not women, not "real" women anyway. They believe we are essentially male, a claim they defend by pointing to our biological features. They divide the human population—all seven billion of us—into one of two mutually exclusive categories: "male" and "female." They ignore intersex people as "anomalous" versions of males and females rather than their own category, which begs the question about how many sexes there are.

They argue that the only way to be a woman is to be female. But what does it mean to be female? GCers often use the definition that females are those creatures that produce eggs and can get pregnant. Trans women do not produce eggs and cannot get pregnant from sperm (though uterus transplants now make it possible for trans women to have a womb), thus trans women are not female and thus not women.

But, you might retort, not all cis females can get pregnant. Many are infertile. Does this mean these cis females are not female? Not women? Here's where things get tricky. GCers fall back on a "normality" clause such that the infertile cis females belong to a class of beings where, if things go "normally" in development, they will be able to get pregnant. Thus females are those beings who "normally" can get pregnant. GCers then argue that this class of beings is globally oppressed on the basis of their biological sex (which normally can get pregnant). If you are of the class that normally can get pregnant, then you are oppressed by virtue of belonging to that class.

But going down this route is philosophically dangerous. The crux of the issue is defining the notion of "normal." Who gets to decide what's normal and what's abornmal? If you say that male and females are "normal" and intersex people/trans/infertile people are "abnormal," how is that judgment made? GCers might try to rely on statistical normality, going by what the "majority" of cases indicate. Trans/intersex people make up probably about 1–2 percent of the total human population. And so we are "abnormal" in this respect.

But why should we rely on a statistical definition of normality? After all it's perfectly consistent to say instead that it's "normal" for intersex people to be born, they are just rare. Rarity does not automatically equate to "abnormal," for the same reason that rare biological traits are not necessarily always pathological. The problem is that normality judgments cannot just be read from nature so easily—there is almost always an element of human subjectivity in trying to define what is to count as "normal."

There's an analogous debate happening about vegetative state patients.[4] Are they people? If we define personhood in terms of consciousness, then vegetative state patients are not people. But we could also say vegetative state patients belong to the class of humans where it is "normal" to have consciousness and that anyone who belongs to that class is a person. See how dangerous "normality" arguments are? They reflect a kind of magical thinking whereby you have a linking property that connects reality to the ideal world of what's "normal."

But vegetative state patients are *not* persons if we define personhood not in terms of normality but in terms of the actual reality of their mental state. The same thing happens in the abortion debate. Pro-lifers say that even if fetuses do not have consciousness, they belong to the class of beings that, if things go normally, will eventually turn into people with consciousness. But the reality is that fetuses are not people—they are clumps of cells with no consciousness.

Similarly, the reality of some cis females not being able to get pregnant cries out for a new definition of womanhood that does not rely on the magical thinking of normality. It doesn't matter if "normally" women can get pregnant because in reality some woman do not have any biological capacity to reproduce and yet they are 100 percent women just the same. So why not say the same thing for trans women? Trans women cannot get pregnant and yet they are women.

The problem with normality arguments is that they are essentialist, trying to find the singular "essence" of womanhood and pinning that down on one category, namely, biological sex. But we know that in reality biological sex is complicated by intersex/trans people—biological reality is not easily cleaved into two categories (male and female) unless you are willing to write off a significant segment of the population as "abnormal" even though there's nothing physically wrong with them in the sense of being more likely to die.

In conclusion, it's philosophically suspect for GCers to try and define womanhood in terms of the biological capacity to get pregnant because it's essentialist nonsense masquerading as legit science when in reality their arguments are not scientific at all but rather ideological. Their first assumption is that trans women

CANNOT be women and then they try to find a definition of womanhood that gives them that conclusion while at the same time arguing they're doing this in order to fight oppression against cis females. But it's not a competition. Trans women are also oppressed by patriarchy—often in the exact same way cis women are. Trans women and cis females are thus natural allies and it saddens me that so many don't understand that. *All* women, trans or otherwise, need to work together and acknowledge our intersecting identities and privileges in order to fight patriarchal oppression.

23

AUTOGYNEPHILIA, THE GIFT THAT KEEPS ON GIVING

Autogynephilia is the gift that keeps on giving, and by "gift" I mean "punch in the face." Autogynephilia is the theory from hell, a literal weapon of the anti-trans brigade to delegitimize trans women and prevent them from transitioning, restrict their access to healthcare, and eradicate their existence from public life. In a nutshell, the "theory" of autogynephilia, or AGP, says that there are two essentially distinct kinds of trans women: those exclusively attracted to men and everyone else. The ones attracted to men are seen as "legit" by the AGP crowd because they are essentially just oppressed femme gay men who are struggling to survive and find men as dating partners.

But what about the trans women who are either bi/pan or exclusively into women? Those people, according to AGP, are just perverted "adult male late transitioners" living out some fetish they have where they get off to the idea of themselves being women. They're freaks. Deviants. Confused, twisted heterosexual men who transitioned merely to get their rocks off and abdicate familial responsibility. Furthermore, according to the larger ideology of the AGP crowd, letting "autogynephiles" transition was a big mistake and has invariably started the new movement of "genderism" which says that you don't have to pass as a cis-normative woman in order to be valid as a woman. Genderism has now led to The Modern Era of trans rights, the "tipping point" so to speak.

Really? That's all I've got to say about AGP. As someone who knows many bi/pan/gay trans women, as someone who is a "late-transitioning" pan trans woman, this "theory" is totally invalid as a plausible description of the dozens of bi/pan/gay trans women I know. Most trans women I know lead boring normal lives like any other boring normal citizens in America. The idea that trans women would spend hundreds of excruciating hours and thousands of dollars getting facial hair removed as part of a "sexual kick" is the most ridiculous idea ever. The idea that trans women would voluntarily put themselves through so much shit merely in order to enhance their sex life is laughable.

Furthermore, from the way the AGP crowd talks you'd think that gay and straight trans women are from two different planets. Yes, some things are statistically different, such as average transition age, with straight trans women transitioning earlier, but the way AGP folks talk you'd think that all trans kids are straight and all trans adults are gay. But the average age for straight trans women to transition is about 30 and for gay trans women it's about 35 or 40, which isn't really all that different. It certainly doesn't suggest they are entirely different species just because of who they are attracted to, which is the only significant difference between the two groups. The AGP crowd likes to talk about how all gay trans women are "pigs in wigs" and all straight trans women are pretty and feminine, but besides this being grossly transphobic, I know many counter-examples to that statement and you just can't read off someone's sexual orientation from their "passability." That's the whole problem with AGP "theory:" it attempts to make massive generalizations about an extremely diverse group of people all based on a simplified account of sexual orientation.

Zinnia Jones and Julia Serano have both dissected and debunked the "science" of autogynephilia in much more detail than I ever aspire to. My point in writing this article is merely to ridicule the theory, to laugh at how absurd it is to say that trans women persist in their transitions merely in order to live out some twisted fantasy. AGP ignores the large swathe of trans women who are simply asexual or who have such low libidos as to be practically asexual. There is nothing sexy about being denied healthcare or being forced to go through the gatekeeping system simply to get access to hormones or life-saving surgery. There is nothing sexy about getting murdered in the street. There is nothing sexy about getting your facial hair removed. There is nothing sexy about facing laughter and ridicule from co-workers, friends, and strangers.

As Serano[5] has explained, many trans women, before they transition, do have what she calls "female embodiment fantasies" but if you were experiencing dysphoria about your gendered body, wouldn't you too have an active imagination that revolved around the idea of having your correct body? And as Jones[6] points out, when you are forced by circumstance to explore your gender in secret behind locked doors there is going to be an element of novelty and excitement that goes away once you have the freedom to be yourself 24/7. Transition and hormones typically transform female embodiment fantasies into what doctors call "mundane reality."

There is nothing especially fun or thrilling about being a bi/pan/gay trans woman in 2018. Sure, it's better than the alternative: being forced to live as a man and suffer your gender dysphoria in silence. But that in no way makes post-transition life some kind of thrill ride of sexual adventure and arousal. The idea that people could think that about such a large and diverse group of women suggests they are not really creating their theory from the data but using propaganda to stigmatize trans women in order to further their political ideology of morally mandating trans women out of existence.

The theory of AGP does actually accurately describe a small segment of the population but it's not gay/bi/pan trans women: it's cis men who self-identify as autogynephiles. Such people do exist. There have been books written about them, chronicling their narratives. A very small percentage of that population does go on to transition but essentially identify as AGP males. But most true AGPers identify as men but have "crossdreaming" fantasies of some kind. Whether or not they'd actually change their bodies to fulfill their fantasy if given the option is another question. And yeah, it's great that some people positively self-identify as AGP. But don't turn around and say it must be true of all trans women either.

AGP just makes no sense as a theory of why trans women go through all the trouble of transition. Could it really be true that the millions of trans women across the world could all be strictly separated into two mutually exclusive groups with no overlap? Could it really be true that the primary reason why trans women transition is either to become "super gay" and attract men or because they want to live out a sexual fantasy? Or, maybe, just maybe, trans women transition for the same reason trans men do (who are *totally* left out of AGP theory building, by the way)—gender dysphoria, the sense of incongruity between your gender identity and your birth assignment. Furthermore, trans women have existed for thousands of years in cultures all around the world—so all that culture is nothing but the product of sexually deviant minds? That would be too incredible.

AGP is the kick in the face that keeps on kicking because it can't be falsified. Any evidence to the contrary is spun into an epicycle and explained away by the trans people being "deceptive" or essentially in bad faith. The AGP crowd has never explained exactly what it would take to prove the theory wrong, even though it does not sit with the available evidence. But it fits into a convenient narrative that is spread by both the gender critical crowd and fundamentalist conservatives: trans women are sexual predators and they shouldn't be allowed in women-only spaces. This is the narrative at the heart of AGP. It's why the theory is so pernicious. AGP and bathroom bills are two sides of the same coin. They are spun from the same fabricated cloth. The only way bathroom bills are going to die is if AGP also dies a painful death.

24

GENDER HACKING, BIO-SEX, AND THE NEW IDENTITY POLITICS

Technology is a site of power in which the human is produced and reproduced.

Judith Butler, Undoing Gender

Trans people are currently in the spotlight of American consciousness. Like never before, trans people are challenging entrenched narratives about gender, politics, and the limits of human freedom. In place of these old narratives are new stories about freedom of expression, freedom of self-exploration, freedom of identity, and the ultimate resilience of the human spirit.

The challenge that trans people bring to the cis world comes not merely from a dialectical shift but from our mere existence. Just being a trans person in 21st-century America is a political statement in its own right. As the saying goes, existence is resistance.

One of the narratives that trans people are challenging is the immutability of biological sex. How is it we define the concepts of "male" and "female?" Typically, it's done in terms of gamete production: males have the developmental capacity for producing small, mobile gametes and females have the developmental capacity for producing large, immobile gametes.

But another conceptual approach to sex is to define the male vs female binary in terms of the developmental capacities that produce the majority of sexual dimorphism in physical and behavioral phenotypes. And when we look at that, the answer is clearly sex hormones: estrogen dominance vs testosterone dominance. Sex hormones determine much of phenotypical, behavioral sexual difference.

So it's not implausible to define the concept of sex in two classes: males are dominated by testosterone and females are dominated by estrogen. And if we think about sex that way, then modern hormone replacement therapy has the technological power to change biological sex because it can take a testosterone-dominant creature and turn them into an estrogen-dominant creature.

Personally, I am agnostic about what the right conceptual framework is for thinking about sex. It kind of seems arbitrary based on our explanatory goals as theorists of the gendered experience. But nevertheless, the fact that trans people are routinely undergoing hormone replacement therapy represents a conceptual and existential threat to entrenched narratives about gender and sex.

And especially now that estrogen and testosterone are available for sale on the black market, practically anyone can obtain these powerful agents of biological change, essentially engaging in a kind of "gender hacking." This shift towards biological self-exploration represents a radical departure from the traditional gatekeeping of yesteryear, where doctors and the medical establishment guarded the resources needed to make fundamental, sexed changes to our bodies.

Just like post-humanists are turning themselves into cyborgs, now pretty much anyone can become a gender cyborg (a person who has used modern synthetic hormones to alter their biophysical make-up for whatever reason). Believe it or not, not everyone who desires to gender hack is doing so for the identity issues typical of trans people. But trans people have made this possibility part of the techno-cultural landscape.

And that's just sex. Trans people are also in the process of uprooting preconceived notions of what it means to belong to a gender class, be it man, woman, or something else. Many trans people are discontent with the category of either "man" or "woman" and seek to carve out another space in-between or outside that traditional binary. The growing acceptance of non-binary people represents another new line of flight into novel gender territory.

But even for a trans person firmly within the classical gender binary, their very existence is a political statement. It cannot be otherwise because many transphobes would like nothing more than for trans people to be eradicated by society by making social and physical transition impossible. Means to accomplish this social genocide are already being enacted, for example outlawing trans people from using the public bathrooms they feel are safe, banning trans people from the military, maintaining the legal status quo that allows trans people to be fired for being trans or transitioning, legally sanctioning housing and medical discrimination, and in general making trans people out to be second-class citizens.

Gay people used to occupy the position trans people do today in terms of being targets for conservative "wedge issues" that drive people to the polls as a distraction from more significant issues. The increased visibility of trans people in the media has only accelerated the cultural scapegoating of trans people.

Yet we are here to stay. We not only have our own thriving culture but we are now part of the American psyche. Unfortunately, that tends to manifest in just us being the butt of jokes (lately there seems to be a steady stream of A-list comedians committed to humiliating trans people for the sake of being "edgy"). But modern identity politics in America can now be largely framed in terms of whether you are "with" trans people or "against" them. They have become a lightning rod for the culture war between "social justice warriors" and everyone else and a proxy for how we define the left vs the right.

And, of course, that culture war in reality represents a complex spectrum of political opinion that is wildly diverse. But nevertheless, trans people have become the go-to thought experiment for thinking about gender, power, and the limits of identity politics. Few people actually know a real-life trans person but almost everyone has an opinion on how we should live our lives.

Transgender ideology has become a dominant culture force in society at the same time trans people are being routinely murdered just for being trans. We represent the bleeding edge of the progressive movement while also being paradoxically in the shadows, being talked over, and having our narratives told by those who have not lived our lives.

But like it or not, trans people have arrived and we're not going anywhere. Things are going to get more intense. The culture war will be accelerated and people will remember this moment in American history.

25

A PLEA FOR AGNOSTICISM IN AN AGE OF ARDOR

A conclusion is what you reach when you get tired
of thinking.

Anonymous

Can we please, as a society, develop our agnosticism muscles a little more?

This country is deeply divided on so many important issues: we are angry and alienated from both each other and ourselves; we live in a post-truth society where fake news is so insidious it's not always clear what's true and what's not; we live inside artificially constructed Facebook bubbles; we don't as individuals have the resources to factcheck everything we read; we know mostly everything we know through endless chains of testimony like a bad game of telephone; we can't tell what's clickbait and what's another day in politics; the algorithms of social media determine what we believe more than our own quest for the truth—we live an age where "truthiness" reigns supreme as the epistemic value of choice.

But who can really blame us? We are after all just naked apes, fragile and error-prone apes at that, who often claim certainty about things we have no right to claim certainty for, who make sweeping philosophical claims with nothing to back them up, who take our experiences and generalize them to everyone and everything else—I mean our consciousness is a barely functioning ever-ready-to-topple piece of gooey machinery scrapped together out of spare parts, a fragile little piece of work that often goes wrong in so many ways.

But it is our home. We ought to respect our home and acknowledge it as a product of evolution, genetics, epigenetics, development, socialization, learning, and so on, and thus susceptible to not getting things exactly right when it comes to knowing the actual real truth of how the universe works or whether some complex philosophical claim is true.

Given what we know about ourselves as being what Nietzsche called "human, all too human," why the hell would we ever claim to know so many things with such strong conviction when we could alternatively just relax a little? I just can't recommend people thinking we know things with strong certainty. I mean, yes, maybe it's certain that $2 + 2 = 4$ but it's a lot more fuzzy on issues such as: does God exist? Is happiness valuable? What is consciousness? What is a soul? Is nihilism false? Is democracy the best system of government? What is the nature of gender?

For any highly contentious subject that offers no clear methodology for settling the matter in a public, falsifiable manner we are left with a situation where eventually in any dialectic we just want to slam our fists down on the table and call it an argument.

The problem here is that strong moral convictions have led to a lot of good in our universe. But at the same time strong moral convictions have also led to a lot of bad. It's nigh impossible to calculate the net effect but I think on the whole relaxing the strength of our convictions a little would still allow for community-benefiting moral truths like "treat others as an end in themselves" to continue to spread while warding off the moral convictions of, for example, transphobes.

Thorough-going agnosticism is not an easy system to adopt fully for it bleeds into our personal lives rather quickly. For example, I have argued for a position I call gender agnosticism. Gender agnosticism is about refusing to make a stand on whether the gender/sex distinction is true or not. Is gender ("womanhood") different from sex ("female")? I can see the arguments on both sides. But there seems to be no way to come to a definitive conclusion that is amenable to public consensus. It's not as if we can build a measuring device and go out into the world to determine if gender is different from sex. If you try to operationalize the concept, you are left with the question: why that particular operationalization? And if we used another, how would we determine which one is better getting at the truth? We'd need a third source. But how do we determine the truth of that one as well? It goes round and round in a circle.

But if I truly believe in gender agnosticism, I cannot even be certain of whether my body is male or female. The lack of positive belief renders my self-awareness devoid of content and I am left with less self-knowledge. But what remains is surely the truth. For what I am left with is the notion that whether I am male or female in an ultimate metaphysical sense is not as important as other things like: people using my pronouns, being treated with dignity and respect, having secure employment, healthcare, housing, and so on. Of course, whether other people believe I am male or female could impact on the lives of trans people by virtue of stigma and the political ramifications of legislation that targets trans bodies.

Does the negative political impact of gender agnosticism render it false? One might think so, assuming a pragmatic epistemology. But in my view, whether gender agnosticism leads to social harm depends on the context of the community in which it's believed. In some communities, it's easy for me to imagine the spread of something like gender agnosticism leading to more freedom and happiness. But in other contexts, it could, of course, be used to harm as well.

I want to be clear that I am not advocating for apathy where we just stop caring about how things are defined or what's true or not true. I care deeply about the truth. I just think it's pretty difficult to arrive at the Ultimate Truth for topics that have some degree of philosophical assumption built in, which is just about every topic imaginable.

We should not stop having dialogue about these tough topics. We should not stop having strong moral convictions. But what drives me crazy is the arrogance of people assuming that they are in possession of the Whole Truth, and not what they actually possess: a distorted fragment. The truth might be out there, but it's quite another thing to assume we have arrived at it in its entirety. The whole of human history shows us being wrong about just about everything—do we really think that early 21st-century humans have finally figured everything out? Chances are we are also really very wrong about a great number of things, many of which would probably be quite embarrassing if in the future we had to stand and be judged in front of our descendants and explain our way of doing things.

So, above all, I advocate for humility in the face of the daunting likelihood that many of the truths we cherish are deeply false. Epistemic humility is a trait that is undervalued in the modern social environment with the virality of media often being tied to the confidence of its proclamations rather than the veracity of its content.

And yes, I am aware that my conclusion renders the whole of this essay less likely to be true. So fair warning: my own arguments for agnosticism could be wrong. Don't assume they're true just because they seem convincing to you now. And if they were never convincing to you in the first place, bravo, you might be right!

26

THERE I GO AGAIN, THINKING I HAVE A BASIC RIGHT TO EXIST IN SOCIETY

There is a shockingly large contingent of Americans who believe that trans women should not have access to women-only spaces like bathrooms, locker rooms, shelters, prisons, women's centers, lesbian spaces, and festivals. I will call this contingent the Birthers, because they usually say things like only females who had "female" checked off on their original birth certificate can have access to women-only spaces, which would prevent trans women from using the bathroom they feel in their best judgment is most appropriate for them.

Ironically, Birthers usually place a very high value on the idea of freedom yet deny trans women the freedom to be themselves. Birthers are gatekeepers, they want to restrict access to life-saving medical treatment such as puberty blockers, hormone replacement surgery, and surgical treatments. They want to absolutely reduce the numbers of children and adults transitioning, socially or medically. For these people, the only acceptable solution to the "trans problem" is a form of conversation therapy, an attempt to mind-fuck trans people into submitting to the fate of their non-consensual birth assignment. The fundamental goal of the Birthers is to eradicate the desire for transition, the possibility of transition, and the pragmatics of transition.

Part of the strategy for inflicting this on trans people is by using propaganda to overly emphasize how gender and thus appropriate social access to gendered facilities is determined by your so-called "innate biological essence." This is often described by Birthers as a "fact" or "reality" that trans people are somehow "delusional" about. But trans people are not delusional. The difference between the body dysmorphic person and the gender dysphoric person is that the dysmorphic person misperceives the nature of their own body, giving it physical properties that don't exist. The gender dysphoric person, in contrast, knows full well the reality of their body, and that knowledge is usually the basis for medically transitioning and a source of the dysphoria itself.

The Birthers are so quick to point to "middle school biology" to solidify their argument but as Dan Dennett once wisely said, "There is no such thing as philosophy-free science—there is only science whose philosophical baggage is taken on board without examination."[7] The question of whether gender is different from sex is not a question that can be answered purely with science—it is a deeply philosophical question resting on complex questions of personal identity and gender as a performative, socially embedded, experiential and subjective phenomenon. As Simone de Beauvoir famously said, "One is not born, but rather, becomes a woman."[8]

Upwards of 60 percent of trans people say they avoid public bathrooms. Without access to public bathroom facilities trans people are actually at risk of damaging themselves by being compelled to hold their bladders for too long for fear of using either the men's room or the women's room. Either option presents real dangers and so for many trans people the reality is that they don't use public restrooms at all. If they walk out of a movie, rather than waiting in line, they might just hold on until they get home. This is just one basic illustration of the way in which Birthers want to see trans folks eradicated from society. They want us to accept our birth assignments as absolute biological destiny and would, if possible, totally restrict the small daily freedoms that allow trans people to exist in public society.

But here's the problem: Birthers will never understand the trans experience. They are not trans and have no concept of what it really means to have an incongruity with your gender. They can't even fathom it. And if they do attempt to get their heads around it, they often just deny that its fundamental basis is true and go on to insist that the morphological shape of genitals we had as babies determines entirely and forever the very complicated phenomenon of our genders and how we fit into society. Talk about reductionist. Talk about rigid, stale, conservative, anti-freedom, anti-justice. They have no appreciation of the arguments in favor of thinking that gender can come apart from physiological properties. Ironically, most Birthers think that consciousness and the soul can come apart from biology but not gender for some reason, though gender is, of course, both a deeply social and deeply subjective phenomenon.

The Birthers are fundamentally just hypocrites hiding behind the social force of tradition. They value religious liberty, but not the liberty of trans people to make decisions about their healthcare, or about which bathroom they should use. Birthers justify this restriction of freedom by referencing the hypothetical possibility that a male person could abuse this freedom in order to harm girls and women. But it's not as if there's a lock on the bathroom door. A cis male can walk in at any time and there is no magic barrier blocking him from entering the bathroom and assaulting a woman or girl.

Bathroom bills are terrible solutions to a non-existent problem. There might be a handful of problematic cases existing out there somewhere. With a population of seven billion humans, and trans people accounting for approximately 1 percent of the population, that makes 71 million trans people across the globe. Out of 71 million trans people, it seems statistically likely for there to be at least *some* bad apples. But let me emphasize there is no empirical evidence showing that trans women commit crimes at a higher rate than cis women. I repeat, no evidence. There is just one misinterpreted Swedish study[9] but the author of the study said herself that nothing about the study suggests that your average trans woman who has transitioned circa 2018 is at any greater risk of being a criminal.

Bathroom bills are not created from the data. They are created from the ideological premise that, as Janice Raymond, the famous "radical feminist" who wrote that trans women are all rapists, said, transgenderism must be morally mandated out of existence. Notice how this fits in line with many religious organizations such as the Roman Catholic church, who have said that trans people represent a grave threat to the moral order of society as dictated by the natural law of God. When your feminism aligns perfectly with what the Pope says about trans people being akin to "nuclear weapons," then I think you need to reconsider your feminism.

Trans people have inalienable rights. We have a right to exist in society how we see fit according to our deepest vision of how we want our lives to go, so long as we respect the autonomy of other people as well and think about the happiness of others. If you do not like the language of inalienable rights, translate it into utilitarianism. As John Stuart Mill wrote, "'To do as you would be done by,' and 'to love your neighbor as yourself,' constitute the ideal perfection of utilitarian morality."[10]

27

SACRED BULLSHIT

A rebuttal to Dan Harris

In 2016, the prestigious literary magazine *The Antioch Review* published an article by Dan Harris called "The Sacred Androgen: The Transgender Debate."[11] This article is deeply transphobic. This essay is my response to Mr. Harris.

Harris's article goes off the rails immediately when he refers to trans people as "TGs." This is objectifying, dehumanizing, othering, and basically makes us sound like a weird class of alien people, setting up the article for its all-encompassing ignorance. Is it really so hard to just say "trans people?"

Harris tries to position himself as a well-meaning but "concerned" ally by saying trans people still have humanity and cites some of the statistics related to our plight. After all, how could Harris be transphobic if he acknowledges that society continues to fuck trans people over? But the tactic is transparent and ultimately fails to make up for the ignorance demonstrated throughout the rest of the piece.

After that quick aside, Harris runs headfirst into some deeply problematic territory. He says that trans people are "entangling" us with pleas for proper pronouns. He calls this plea "Byzantine" and "patronising" and a "snare." Yes, my desire to not be called "he" or "sir" is so complex and patronizing (and he's not even talking about non-binary pronouns). I'm sorry our desires to not be misgendered are so inconvenient for cis people like yourself, Mr. Harris. You must really spend so much time agonizing over how badly trans people treat you because we ask you to use our pronouns. How many trans people have you met, Mr. Harris? How many times have you actually had to think about pronoun usage? Does this really pose a problem in your life? Compare that with how troubling it is for a trans person to be routinely misgendered—it literally feels like a knife in the gut, one that is jabbed in and out day in, day out, for years. And yet my desire to not be knifed in the gut is "Byzantine."

Next, Harris says it's "insulting" to use the "pejorative" term "cisgender." He defines it as "those of us who accept, however unenthusiastically, our birth gender." But this is wrong. It's not about enthusiasm or comfort or anything like that, nor is it about "accepting your birth gender." It literally means "non trans." Mr. Harris, are you a trans person? If not, then you're cis. It's not an insult. It's a description. It's not meant to define your entirety as a person, you are surely more than just a mere Not Trans Person. I mean, it's in the *Oxford English Dictionary*. It's used by academics. It's completely neutral. The only reason it feels like an insult is because it's not a term you would choose to describe yourself because you don't identify as "not trans." But tough luck.

According to Harris, trans people shouldn't be upset that cis people are "curious" about our bodies. But the fact that Harris can't see the problem with this curiosity just hammers home the cis blinders that Harris has on. Of course, he fails to see the problem, because Harris has never been reduced to just his genitals, or been gawked at like a freakshow, or had a horrible time dating because of people rudely asking about his private parts. You know who else is curious? Kids are curious about why someone has a scar or birthmark on their face but guess what? We teach them to be polite and not bring it up unless the context is right. Why can't Mr Harris learn that simple lesson when it comes to people's genitals?

Furthermore, Harris complains that trans people "ridicule" the blunders cis people make when dealing with trans people. Really? Would you say black folks are "ridiculing" white folks for their racism or merely pointing out all the ways white people have been fucking up?

Harris's prime example of trans people running amok? Janet Mock correcting a talk show host for saying she was "born a boy." How horrible! A trans woman trying to create some space for linguistic nuance in order to correct systematic cis-sexist assumptions about the nature of gender identity—yup, truly horrible.

Mr. Harris is upset that trans people are attempting to "dictate the terms of the debate" with our bullying. But I cannot apologize that our attempts at controlling our own narrative are so irksome to you. Yes, because it's not as if disability activists are doing the same thing. Or anti-racism activists are doing the same thing. Marginalized people have always sought to define the terms of their own debate because if we don't do it for ourselves then the non-marginalized folks will do it for us, and we all know how great they are at doing that. Mr. Harris is upset because cis people are "thinkers" too and their opinions are just as valid as those of trans folks. Except they are really not. Just like a black person is better positioned to point out racism, a trans person is better positioned to point out transphobia.

Harris continues to display his bigotry openly. He writes: "the whole phenomenon of switching one's gender is a mass delusion."

Harris's first argument for trans being a delusion is that society apparently disapproves of plastic surgery. Which is news to me. But anyway, the argument is that society makes fun of celebrities who have too much plastic surgery. And Harris tries to make the analogy that gender surgery is simply akin to plastic surgery, the bad kind, the "superficial, cosmetic" kind.

But wait, has Harris thought this through? A better analogy for trans surgery is corrective plastic surgery such as a person without a nose receiving plastic surgery to make their face look more normal, or surgery to correct a cleft palate. Sure, it's just about "appearances" but when your appearance is so deeply tied into your psychological well-being because you are tired of being stared at in public like a freak it's no longer "merely cosmetic." Look, trans people sometimes kill themselves because their anguish with their bodies is so great. That is nothing like a celebrity getting a fifth nose job.

Harris also alludes to Michael Jackson making himself white (I will not get into how wrong Harris is about Jackson's reasons for undergoing those treatments) and says that one is "self-mutilation" but the other is justified. Harris's essential problem here is that because he is cis he can't imagine a motive for wanting facial feminization surgery that isn't shallow. Just as he can't imagine what it's like to have gender dysphoria. He can't imagine the mental anguish that having a prominent brow-bone causes some trans women or the pain and anguish of trans men having to bind their chests. If he can't see the essential humanity and justness of performing surgeries to alleviate such suffering, then he is the deluded one—the one who cannot exercise basic empathy for people with different fundamental needs.

Furthermore, he tries to make an analogy between celebrity plastic surgery and trans people taking hormones. The disanalogy is so obvious that I won't belabor the point but clearly Harris is grasping at straws. Furthermore, his whole premise is that society looks down on plastic surgery so we should also look down on trans surgery. But the premise is false. Plastic surgery is widely accepted as normal and healthy. A 50-year-old woman having a face lift is perfectly normal; she is not seen as a pariah. A woman having breast implants is not universally scorned by society. Harris is confusing the disdain we have for people having excessive plastic surgery with the acceptance we have with people having appropriate plastic surgery to simply make themselves happier in their bodies.

In a nutshell, Harris is reviving the old radical feminist trope about body modification being immoral. I won't belabor the point because all we need to do is point to the value of autonomy in American society to realize that actually bodily autonomy and body modification are perfectly acceptable to Americans. So saying that we must accept our bodies as they are at birth is deeply conservative and not at all in line with an ethical system that says it is ok for us to autonomously modify our bodies so long as we are not hurting other people. The increasing popularity of tattoos among middle-class professionals proves my point.

Harris brings up "evidence" that some trans women get breast implants that are apparently too large for him to approve of. Did he do his research on trans women from watching porn? How many trans women does he know? The number of trans women who don't want super large breast implants vastly outweighs the number of trans women that do, yet Harris does not highlight that because it does not fit into his narrative of trans women just being superficial caricatures of femininity, a TERF trope that goes all the way back to Raymond's *The Transsexual Empire*.[12] But in order to debunk this trope all it takes is...wait for it... actually getting to know the diversity of the trans community and knowing how many trans women do not want to be caricatures of femininity and the many trans women who have butch or tomboy gender expressions, just like cis women. But no, Harris only chooses to engage with a stereotype because that's what he's learned from watching cis media or from his own personal experiences.

And notice also how this attack is only against trans women. Where is the critique of trans men hitting the gym in order to beef up and attain a superhero body? Yeah, that's not problematic, yet trans women wanting a bigger butt is somehow deeply so. Once again, Harris cherry-picks his anecdotes to reinforce stereotypes about the contrived and over-zealous femininity of trans women, which belies the truth and also conveniently ignores trans masculine people.

Harris seems to pick up his "knowledge" of the True Trans Experience by watching exploitative TV journalism such as the TV show *Botched*. Watching TV is so much easier than actually going out and interviewing hundreds of trans women in order to form a representative sample of such a diverse community. Where else does Harris get his knowledge of what trans women are really like? Craigslist. Seriously. He cites Craigslist. But anyone who has been on Craigslist knows that the types of trans people on Craigslist are not representative of the general community, since most trans people are smart enough to realize that Craigslist is creepy and bordering on fetishistic.

Harris is just regurgitating classic TERF ideology: the idea that if only society was more liberal about gender expression, then trans people wouldn't feel the need to transition and take hormones or have surgery. Harris assumes that if only men were allowed to wear dresses, then trans people wouldn't exist. This is incredibly naive and has been debunked by trans scholars time and time again. Even if some trans folks do transition because of wanted freedoms in gender expression, the vast majority of trans folks have issues with their bodies not their clothing.

And besides, suppose a trans woman wanted to transition simply because she wanted the freedom to have long hair, wear women's clothing and makeup. Do you know how weird it would be to essentially pass as a woman yet for everyone including yourself to think of you as a man? Like it or not we just do not live in a society where men can pass as women yet function in society as a man. If you pass as a woman, then it makes perfect sense why you would want to switch pronouns and legally change your name. It would also make perfect sense why you would want hair removal and hormones because if you are wearing women's clothing and you still look like a man, then your chances of being violently attacked or harassed go way up. But all that is besides the point because most trans people do not transition because of gender expression—it's usually about our bodies or our deep-seated sense of identity, and the clothing is usually secondary.

Harris pushes for "androgyny" as the ideal state of human gender expression, somehow insinuating that this is what True Feminism advocates for. But clearly Harris knows nothing about the power of women and men and non-binary folks to reclaim the power of femininity as a genuine mode of authentic self-expression.

On to trans kids. Harris claims that more and more parents are pushing their kids to transition when they show the "slightest hint" of gender non-conformity. What planet does Harris live on? Where oh where are there parents eager for their kids to transition? That is not reality. Most parents would do anything *other* than encourage their kid to transition. Harris is just plain wrong on this front and perpetuates a dangerous talking point about trans kids—that there would be fewer trans kids if we simply let kids explore their gender expression. But the truth is that most parents who "let" their kid transition are doing it because they see the extreme anguish their kid would experience if they did not allow it. Harris is under the false delusion that parents are "badgering" their kids to transition when in fact it's the opposite: it's the kids doing the badgering and the parents reluctantly going along.

Harris claims, absurdly, that children begin hormone therapy as young as four. That's so wildly inaccurate that I have no reason to trust anything else Harris says on the matter. Most trans kids go on puberty blockers in their teens before they start hormone therapy.

Harris talks about the problems of the "trapped in the wrong body" metaphor without any appreciation of how modern trans discourse is moving away from that metaphor, with most trans folks I know saying how it is wrong to use it to apply to all trans folks because many do not feel that it is appropriate. But because Harris gets all his knowledge of trans folks from cis media he doesn't appreciate the nuances of discourse within the trans community.

Harris gets philosophical critiquing the mind–body problem with respect to the metaphor without appreciating how trans folks often relied on this metaphor because (1) explaining dysphoria to cis people is difficult and (2) it became an acceptable way to get past gatekeeping nonsense in order to get access to HRT and surgery. It become a cliche even within the trans community because we needed a way to pass the hurdles of gatekeeping therapists and doctors and that metaphor is one the professionals would accept.

Harris waxes philosophical like a stoner in college about how trans people are really just creating another problem. He asks, naively, "Why is one gender better than the other?" *It just is!* That's the nature of dysphoria. But Harris's cis blinders prevent him from understanding or empathizing with gender dysphoric individuals. He writes, "In being true to themselves, aren't they being false to their own bodies?" Um, it's the other way around. Their body is *false*. The body is the problem. The body is what is causing the pain and the anguish. Harris can't understand that because his own body seems so normal and obviously why would it be wrong for *him* to reject his male body?

Harris tries to argue that gender transition is pointless because "An attempted suicide rate of a staggering 41 percent suggests that many TGs experience profound disillusion over the fact that their problems were not resolved during their transition." But Harris simply hasn't done his research. If he had made any attempt at research beyond watching reality TV or surfing Craigslist, he would have discovered that gender transition, especially medical transition, is correlated with lower rates of suicide below the 41 percent number and, furthermore, the research shows that most suicidal ideation and depression stems from transphobia, not being trans itself. The research shows clearly that when trans people have safe, supportive, loving environments to transition in, their mental health is roughly the same as that of the cisgender population. Harris writes, "If TGs initiated this journey to find mental health, there is no evidence whatsoever that they achieve it." How did this pass peer review? "No evidence whatsoever" means that Harris couldn't spend ten minutes on Google Scholar looking it up. There is plenty of evidence, Mr. Harris, but it helps to not begin your research with the conclusion in mind.

I can't go on. There is so much BS in the Harris article I'm afraid it would take dozens more pages to deconstruct everything problematic in the article. And this is just an essay, not a scholarly engagement. But I hope my counter-review reveals the essential problem with Harris and his deeply transphobic hit piece: it's based on stereotypes and a lack of knowledge about the diversity of the trans community. Almost everyone likes to think that, oh, I met a trans woman last week, or, oh, I watched a documentary on TV last week, so therefore I can talk confidently about "TGs." But once again the article was a hit piece on trans women. No mention of trans men at all, of course. TERFs somehow don't realize that trans men exist in equal numbers to trans women. And no mention of non-binary folks. It's a common tactic of TERFs to focus merely on trans women as the "problem" with transgenderism, so much so that many call TERFs "TWEFs," standing for Trans Woman Exclusionary Feminist, because so many radical feminists only seem to have problems with trans women, but say nothing about the parallel of trans men or non-binary folks.

This is an old strategy. There is nothing new in Harris's article. He just simply rehashes the same tired talking points from Raymond's 1979 *The Transsexual Empire*. The only thing new in the Harris piece is the pop culture from which Harris derives his stereotypes of trans people. I mean, seriously, he uses his experience in AOL chatrooms to speak authoritatively about the nature of trans women.

The Antioch Review should be ashamed of itself for publishing such a poorly researched and ultimately hateful article. But as Julia Serano predicted, the trans backlash against this article is going to be chalked up to "extreme trans activists," bullying academics, and stifling academic free speech. But we are just trying to take control of our own narrative, to fight back against the stereotypes and accusations of "mass delusion." Harris claims to be "supportive" of the right for trans people to transition but ultimately his article is just another attempt by cis people to discourage transition, something cis people have been doing since forever.

METAPHYSICS AND EPISTEMOLOGY

28

AGAINST THE SEX/ GENDER DISTINCTION

This essay is about the sex/gender distinction. I will argue that the distinction is pernicious, both conceptually and politically, and we should abandon it.

What is the sex/gender distinction? I find the easiest way to illustrate the distinction is with the example of trans people. If you believe in the sex/gender distinction, you might describe a trans woman as having a male sex but a female gender (assuming they identify along the gender binary). Under this schema, it becomes possible to describe a trans woman as having "male parts," "male chromosomes," and so on, but a "female" gender. In the sex/gender distinction, "sex" is also described as one's "biological sex" or "physical sex" and "gender" is described as one's "gender identity" or "psychological sex."

I want to reject this way of thinking altogether. In the view I am advancing in this essay, there is nothing "male" about a trans woman—the term "male" is simply not appropriate as applied to trans women.[1] They don't have "male" body parts because only males have male body parts and in my view trans women are not males but females, so any body part or physical characteristic they have is only appropriately described as female. In my view a trans woman's "physical sex" is female, not male.

I recognize that this might be seen as a "radical" view but let me flesh it out more.

The essential problem comes from the attempt to gender or sex body parts. In my view, there are deep problems with trying to gender body parts. Consider elbows. There are no such things as "male elbows" or "female elbows"—there are just elbows. Likewise, there are no female noses. Or male ears. At a deep, metaphysical level, it just doesn't make a lot of sense to gender body parts like noses or elbows—all we can do is describe their physical characteristics such as size, shape, and texture. I want to say the same thing about every other body part as well. Penises are not "male" because some women have penises. Vaginas are not "female" because some men have vaginas. XY chromosomes are not "male" because some women have XY chromosomes and some men have XX chromosomes.

But someone might say this position is ignoring basic biology or ignoring science. But are the concepts "male" and "female" really necessary scientific concepts or are they extra-empirical concepts that import sexist and transphobic beliefs from an earlier culture? Suppose you described a nose in complete physiological detail using purely scientific vocabulary. At what point would you need to *also* specify whether the nose is male or female in order to give a complete physical description? What does that contribute to scientific understanding? Can we not get all we need out of biology without gendering body parts?

Someone might say that the sex/gender distinction is empirical—that is, we've just gone out and observed all the males and females and come up with the sex/gender distinction in that way. But suppose we knew absolutely nothing about male and female humans and wanted to do an empirical study on the nature of males and females. If we *started* with the assumption that trans women are really women, we wouldn't come to the conclusion that only males have penises or that if you have a penis you must be male. Because trans girls are girls, a trans woman's penis is a "girl's penis," not a male part.

In other words, we can't assume that the sex/gender distinction is perfectly objective because the assumptions we bring to the empirical study change the nature of the conclusion. If we start with the "radical" notion that trans women are really women, then we will not come to the conclusion that XY chromosomes are a bodily trait only associated with males or that penises are "male" body parts.

This perspective also calls into question the language of female-assigned-at-birth feminists describing themselves as "female-bodied." Having breasts and a vagina does not mean you have a "female" body because there are trans men who have that body configuration.

Dismantling the sex/gender distinction also calls into question the infamous "gingerbread person" model of sex and gender which implies one's "sex" is determined by what's between your legs. In the gingerbread model, a trans women would have a female gender but a male sex. But what if that person has gender confirmation surgery, would they thereby change sex? No. The better explanation is that the trans woman already has a female sex and gender confirmation surgery merely brings her body more into alignment with her desires.

One remaining question that I don't have time to discuss here is: how should we think about the concept of "physical sex" applied to non-human animals?

OK so that's the conceptual problem with the sex/ gender distinction. Now let's examine the dangerous political consequences of upholding the distinction.

Consider the recent Houston Equal Rights Ordinance (HERO) that was overwhelmingly rejected by voters. The ordinance attempted to introduce anti-discrimination policies in the city along multiple dimensions but the anti-HERO protesters focused almost exclusively on trans women and bathrooms. The anti-LGBT campaign basically used the tactic of painting trans women as dangerous sexual predators who are going to attack or rape women in women's bathrooms—or they tried to argue that men will take advantage of the HERO rule to put on a dress in order to prey on women in bathrooms while claiming to be trans. The slogan of the anti-HERO campaign was "No Men in Women's Bathrooms." This highly effective campaign was blasted all over the media and ultimately led to the defeat of HERO.

The obvious thing to say here is that the act of a man putting on a dress and walking into the women's room with the explicit intention of causing a disturbance or attacking a woman is already illegal according to local law. So the scenario that anti-HERO protesters are "worried" about is already illegal—the HERO ruling wouldn't thereby interfere with enforcing those laws. The anti-HERO campaign is fear-mongering at its finest. But I want to probe a little deeper and examine how the sex/ gender distinction makes it easier to discriminate against trans people, especially trans women, on the basis of their bodies.

I believe that the sex/gender distinction makes it easier for legislators to write bathroom bills. If you write a bill that says "no men are allowed in the women's restroom," you have to define what it means to be a man and a woman. How is this done? Usually in terms of chromosomes, or genitals, or what it says on your original birth certificate. In other words, the bathroom bills are written in such a way as to exclude trans women from the women's room. Legislators are able to appeal to the idea of one's "biological sex" or "physical sex" and use that to define what it means to be a man or a woman. If there was no distinction between sex and gender, then it would be harder to ban trans women from the women's room on the basis of one's "physical sex." But only with the sex/gender distinction in place does it become possible to write anti-trans legislation that attempts to discriminate specifically against trans people on the basis of their bodies.

Philosophers might intuitively feel repulsed by the idea that I am arguing for the abandonment of an idea because of its political consequences. But in the spirit of pragmatism I reject the notion that we shouldn't consider the political and social consequences of our conceptual schemes. Indeed, this might be the *most important* dimension along which to evaluate certain concepts, especially if they intersect with real-life oppression happening every day, which "gender" definitely does.

P.S. I want to acknowledge that I owe both of these arguments to the excellent Zinnia Jones.

29

TRANS WITHOUT TRANSITION?

A critique of gender identity

I think many people fail to realize that the very idea of "gender" and "gender identity" as opposed to physiological sex is a modern concept, invented by mid-20th century psychiatrists working with gender dysphoric trans patients. Robert Stoller famously defined gender identity as "one's sense of being a member of a particular sex."[2] The concept is best illustrated by trans people, where a person assigned male at birth could have the "opposite" gender identity of being a woman which stands in contrast to her male birth assignment and the gendered expectations associated with that assignment. A classic example of a trans person seeking comfort in their identity is Jan Morris, who wrote in her memoir *Conundrum*, "All I wanted was liberation, or reconciliation—to live as myself, to clothe myself in a more proper body, and achieve Identity at last."[3]

Cis people fail to be amazed about their comfort in their assigned sex. Like the old joke about fish not knowing what water is, cis people often fail to realize that their own felt sense of gender is actively at work behind the scenes, filtering their desires and perceptions. In contrast, trans people, especially pre-transition trans people, feel the mismatch between their gender and birth assignment so acutely it can lead to constant negative rumination, depression, anxiety, and suicidal thoughts.

But what does it mean exactly to "sense" one's membership in a particular sex? What kind of sense is this? Is it like proprioception? Or like the visual sense? Can we just "see" our gender clearly or does it require an act of hermeneutics? Are we constantly sensing our sex? Or is it only evident in gender dysphoric people where there is a mismatch? This is like the old philosophical problem called the "refrigerator light problem" whereby we use introspection to ask ourselves if we are conscious, but are we conscious when we are not thinking about being conscious?

If we were not conscious, we would not know it either way, just like we cannot know if the refrigerator light goes off after shutting the door—the act of investigating corrupts the process of inquiry. It's the same with gender identity. Is it a construction made each time anew when we reflect on our gender or is it a stable psychological foundation that exists when we aren't reflecting?

What is the nature of gender identity? Can it "stand alone" by itself or does it need to be connected to other psychological states such as desires? Presumably gender identity is a type of belief—we have a belief we either belong or don't belong to the male–female gender binary as assigned to us at birth. With trans people, is it merely enough to have the belief that one is a different gender in order to be trans? Or must the belief be connected to a desire to transition?

A thought experiment: imagine an assigned male at birth trans person who wakes up one day and has a startling reali-zation—they are transgender! But they have zero desire to engage in any act of transition. They don't want to change their name, their pronouns, their dress, their mannerisms, their voice, their body. They are totally fine in the gender role assigned to them at birth. Yet they have an internal sense of belonging to the class of females. Is this situation even conceptually possible? Remember: the idea is not that one has a desire to change and is pragmatically frustrated but that there is no desire in the first place. All that exists is a free-floating belief that one is a different gender from the gender one was assigned at birth.

Presumably if gender identity is a coherent concept, then this situation is possible (ignoring for now the problem in assuming that metaphysical possibility can be read off conceptual possibility).

Some trans theorists implicitly assume that to be trans is to transition in some way. Paul Preciado writes:

> In the middle of the Cold War, a new ontological-political distinction between "cis-" (a body that keeps the gender it was assigned at birth) and "trans" (a body availing itself of hormonal, surgical, prosthetic, or legal technologies to change that assignment) made its appearance.[4]

Preciado just flat out assumes that if you are trans, then you are "availing" yourself of some kind of transitional technology to change or move away from your birth assignment. If you are a trans man, that might mean wearing a binder, or a packer, or an STP (stand to pee) device, starting testosterone, and so on. If you're a trans woman, that might mean shaving your body or starting HRT, buying clothes traditionally found in the women's section, and so on. For a non-binary person, it might involve changing your name and pronouns, binding your chest, or wearing different styles of clothing.

But is my thought experiment actually conceptually incoherent? If the idea of "gender identity" is to make sense in its own right, then it should be possible for there to be a trans person with a mismatched gender identity but with no desire to transition in any way. Or perhaps it is impossible—if it is, then it shows that there is something wrong with the idea of gender identity as distinct from physiological sex. It is not enough to simply have an identity that is different from one's assigned identity— one must also have accompanying psychological states such as desires, desires for change, for transition through presentational, hormonal, surgical means.

I believe it is true that to be trans means more than just to have a different identity. It means, as Preciado assumes, but never argues for, that to be trans means to transition. There is no trans-gender without transition. One "transes" one's own gender when one decides to self-consciously move away from one's birth assignment. In a sense, the accompaniment of desires is a confirmation that the identity is not a fleeting whim or a random thought produced by the unconscious. The persistence of desire is in fact one of the defining diagnostic criteria for gender dysphoria.

Notice, however, that transition does not necessarily entail transition to medically relieve bodily dysphoria. The transitional elements could be done for some people without the assistance of medical technology. But availing oneself of legal technologies is certainly a valid and "complete" transition tool. Just simply to have one's governmental ID match one's felt sense of identity is a powerful feeling of validation. Furthermore, the position I'm putting forward is ecumenical between the "trans-medicalists," who argue that being trans is a medical condition defined by bodily dysphoria, and "maximals," who want to expand the trans umbrella to be as inclusive as possible even for those trans people who don't identify as gender dysphoric.

For Preciado's definition, bodily dysphoria is not the defining feature of trans identities. Rather, it is the desire to use multiple forms of transitional technology to reject one's birth assignment. If a non-binary person is happy enough to bind and legally change their name, then that's a form of transition. But where my position draws the line is with self-identified trans people who have no desire to move away from their birth assignment.

But what's the limit? If a trans person merely "transitions" through changing their gendered expression, is that enough to count as trans? I think the problem with trying to police gendered identities in this way is that we cannot from the third person realize the full psychological significance that expression has for different people. For some butch women, getting a short haircut might be no big deal but for a trans boy it might mean the world. The same expressions can mean vastly different things to different people. For some people, the significance invested in how clothing is coded might be enough to satisfy latent dysphoria such that other transitional technologies are unnecessary.

The point is that any kind of gatekeeping that tries to definitely say where "true trans" ends and begins will come up with the problem of trying to legislate from the outside the internal felt sense of significance certain gendered activities have for some people. We will never be able to definitely build a single set of criteria and apply them to all trans people, picking out a unique shared characteristic. Trans people are perhaps one of the most diverse populations on the planet. I propose there is no "essence" to being trans, no necessary and sufficient conditions that are universal across all trans people. Instead, being trans is a family resemblance concept, a cluster concept that works in terms of paradigms, not necessary and sufficient conditions.

In conclusion, being trans is not just about identity. It's about identity and desire. If there is identity without desire, it is passive, but desire without identity is blind.

30

HOW DO I KNOW I AM TRANS?

How do I know I am trans? It's an interesting question, and not at all obvious. Clearly my knowledge of my transness cannot come from mere external observation. There is no clear empirical evidence in the same way I know my height or my weight. For knowledge of my weight I simply step on the scales. But how do I know I am trans? It's not the same type of self-knowledge such as knowing I am hungry. In the stomach, there are nerve endings that can detect my hunger levels which then send those signals to my brain, which interprets them and I gain self-knowledge of my hunger. But my gender identity is not clearly physiological in the same way. There is no instrument, to my knowledge, which can be pointed at my brain to determine my gender with certainty.

Gender is essentially a subjective process, known only through introspection. The only known way for others to know my gender is for me to tell it to them. They cannot read it from my dress or my behavior or whatever. Such things do not deliver gender conclusively, though they can certainly be clues. Is that where my own knowledge of my gender comes from? Observation of many many clues and then inductively piecing together the conclusion that I am trans? Or does my trans knowledge come from a more direct introspective source in the same way I just "directly" know whether I am in pain? I don't have to infer that I am in pain, I just know I am in pain. Similarly, do I just know I am trans? Or do I have to infer it?

In my own case, and all I can do here is speak for myself, my trans knowledge certainly seems more like an inference than it does direct knowledge. I've never "felt like a woman trapped in a man's body." I didn't have a clear and distinct female identity in childhood. It's never been something that is obvious to me. It was a hard-fought introspective battle to reach my current state of knowledge regarding my trans identity.

To this day, my own gender is not obvious to me. I have proclaimed before that I am gender agnostic: I claim no certain knowledge about my own gender. Am I a special type of man or a special type of woman? I do not know. It does not seem important to me. What matters more is self-knowledge concerning my desires to continue transition. I desire to keep using female pronouns, shopping in the women's section, taking HRT, using the name "Rachel," and so on.

Just like I am aware of my desire for food, I am aware of my desire to keep transitioning. This is the knowledge that grounds my knowledge of myself as trans. I know I am trans because I know I never want to go back to being a testosterone-based creature. I know I love estrogen. I know getting gendered as female by other people makes me extremely happy and being perceived as male/man makes me extremely unhappy.

But I didn't always know that I loved estrogen. Before I transitioned, I did not have certain knowledge that I would love estrogen. So how did I gain enough self-knowledge about my desires in order to be confident enough to start transitioning? In early spring 2015 I was exploring my gender-bending and crossdressing more and more, taking things to the next level in terms of trying to pass and going out in public. The feeling was intoxicating. I'll never forget the feeling of walking my dog around the block in a dress for the first time. I was hooked. I didn't want to stop dressing in femme, but I also didn't want to interact with the world as a man with a male name and a male body, being seen by everybody as a crossdresser or pervert. And let's be honest, few groups of people in this country are more derided than male crossdressers. In my opinion, if you are not part of the drag community, it is harder to be an out and about public crossdresser than it is to be a trans woman. The reason is that trans women usually go on hormones in an attempt to blend into society. But if you're a male crossdresser, you are stuck trying to pass with your AMAB body and unless you are very lucky, it's going to be difficult to blend in without doing all the things associated with transition such as facial hair removal and HRT.

So I had a choice. Try to subvert traditional gender roles in an attempt to be an openly crossdressing male or adopt a trans identity and transition, blending into society as a woman-identified person. I think I made the right choice. The longer I transition, the more confident I am that I did the right thing for my happiness and well-being. Never again do I have to choose between expressing my masculine self vs my feminine self. I never have to hide my femininity in the closet again. I never again have to feel ashamed of my femininity. I have the freedom to be exactly who I want to be and no one is stopping me. It's a wonderful feeling, the feeling of liberation from the gender role I was assigned at birth, liberated from the body I was born with, free from the thought patterns I was socialized to think, free from the shackles of masculinity. I can be feminine!

It's surprising to me just how deep my desire for femininity runs. It's part of my DNA, part of my deep wiring. While it is possible that I could have lived a life as a very feminine male, I do not think I would have been able to express myself in the same way I have unless I had fully transitioned to take on a female identity, with female pronouns and a female name. When I think of my birth name it gives me a strange sensation, like having a ring of familiarity but still seeming quite estranged. I can't imagine that I would have lasted long if I had tried to live life as a feminine male. Femme males are chewed up and spit out by society. They are torn down, beaten down, and sometimes even killed. Though I don't pass perfectly and thus expose myself to a similar risk of being clocked as a man in drag and thus a target for violence, I blend well enough that if I keep my mouth closed, I can pass as a woman in society without raising too many eyebrows. This gives my existence a kind of security that I otherwise wouldn't have if I had tried to express myself without transitioning.

Deep down I am a gender agnostic. I do not know with confidence if I am male or female, man or woman. But I do know I am femme. I am a femme person, that much is clear. But it's so much easier to be femme with a government ID that has a female name and "F" on it. It's so much easier to be femme with the help of HRT. It's so much easier to be femme if I tell the world I am trans. Which is not to say that being trans is an easy path, or without its own set of inherent problems. Being trans is no walk in the park. It can be a hard life. But it is also very rewarding. I get to experience the joy of self-determination, the joy of picking a pathway and walking down it with my head held high, the joy of having a vision for how I want my life to go and being able to follow it. It's an indescribable feeling. Cis people can, of course, have the same feeling when they choose a career or whatever, but gender transition is an example par excellence of autonomy and self-actualization. Trans people fight against so much just to be true to their deep inner selves. They make so many sacrifices, giving up friends, family, and career opportunities just for the chance of authenticity.

So, for me, I know I am trans because I have knowledge of my desires. This allows me to make a grand inference: whatever my gender is, it's different from the gender I was assigned at birth. Thus, I am trans.

31

BRAINS, VATS, AND RADICAL FEMINISM

Gender critical feminists (henceforth "GCers")[5] are often skeptical about a concept foundational to trans theory: gender identity, the sense of whether we belong to a particular sex/gender or not. GCers are critical of the very idea of having one's gender be based on your identity as opposed to being grounded in the biological properties of your body. Thus, GCers often define "woman" as an "adult female" where "female" means having certain biological properties such as the capacity to bear eggs, or having the developmental program of egg-production in your DNA make-up, or something like that.

But imagine that a GCer named Janice is asleep one night and a group of evil trans neuroscientists decide to kidnap her and whisk her away to a lab; her brain is extracted from her body and placed in a vat where the biological functions of her brain are supported by a totally artificial body. All that is left of Janice is her brain. No vagina. No breasts. No ovaries or uterus. No capacity whatsoever to make eggs or get pregnant. In many ways, her "body" is not gendered at all: it's just a hunk of brain tissue hooked up to machines. An outside observer would have a hard time determining what the brain's gender is without knowing its past history as Janice. Furthermore, the evil trans neuroscientists are clever enough to provide artificial stimulation to the brain so that it falsely believes that it actually has a body and is interacting with the world in a normal fashion. Much like Neo being inside the Matrix, Janice would not necessarily "feel" like anything other than her normal self.

What happens to Janice's sense of identity as a woman now? She once defined her womanhood entirely in terms of biological features, which no longer exist. How can she hold on to them? Let's assume she is given a theoretical knowledge of herself as a brain-in-a-vat by the evil neuroscientists. Perhaps she reasons that her brain still contains the DNA that carries the information needed to reconstruct those body parts she identified with. But in my opinion, that's a terribly flimsy sense of identity, being tied to the mere potential of the DNA in your body to produce something that doesn't exist. That's a negative identity, based on that which does not exist. It seems unlikely to be the basis for a strong sense of identity as a man or a woman.

One might think that the GCer would just say that her brain is sexed as female, that she has a "female brain" but the irony is that GCers typically are skeptical of the very concept of brain sex, because brain sex is a foundational concept in trans theory. The most common and mainstream explanation of trans identities is the mismatched brain sex explanation whereby a trans woman might say she needs to transition because she was born with a female brain in a male body. This mismatch of brain and body causes gender dysphoria and since we are infinitely more capable of changing the body than the brain, the preferred treatment of both the patients and the doctors is to allow a gender/sex transition that helps realign brain and body by changing the body.

GCers want to morally mandate trans people out of existence and prevent as many transitions as possible so they are opposed to the idea that there is even such a thing as a "female brain" or a "male brain" because that seemingly provides sufficient medical explanation for why transition is necessary. GCers typically believe that male and female brains are only different in so far as they are influenced by society. Otherwise they start off as identical but end up producing different behaviors because they are socialized to do so.

Personally, I feel like any legitimate answer to the nature vs nurture question of sex/gender will probably include at least some nature. In practically all other animal systems in nature there are evolved adaptations in males and females that make their brains distinct in at least some small way—it seems incredible to me that humans could be the drastic exceptions to the entire scheme we see in nature. While yes, it is plausible that nurture is very, very important for the development of brains, it is equally likely that our evolutionary history also plays an important role in the sex differentiation of the body, including the brain.

The latest science suggests, however, that there is more overlap between male and female brains than difference and that your average female brain is composed of not just "female" parts but also many "male" parts. Each of our brains is a mosaic of male and female parts. But in trans people the mosaic is arranged in such a way as to radically mismatch with the body, suggesting that some people's internal cognitive representation of the sex can be aligned so significantly with one gender/sex that it generates gender dysphoria.

Going back to Janice, my feeling is that Janice's sense of womanhood would be as strong as ever as a brain-in-a-vat. In fact, I would wager that her sense of womanhood would remain almost entirely unchanged. Even if she has an abstract sense of herself as being a brain-in-a-vat, the internal representations in combination with the artificial stimulation inside her brain fully determine her subjective experience, including her felt sense of identification as an adult female or woman. But without actually owning a vagina or a womb, can Janice's claim to womanhood be based on anything other than what trans theorists call gender identity?

This is the great irony of Janice's predicament: in order to maintain her sense of womanhood, Janice's brain must be creating an internal representation of which sex/gender she belongs to and an alignment of that representation with the artificial inputs giving her a sense of body. But that internal representation is precisely what trans theorists mean when they talk about "brain sex" and "gender identity"—it's the brain's way of telling itself what gender/sex it should belong to, a sense we all have in some way or another, even if that sense is telling us we don't belong to any gender (a-gender).

32

GENDER AGNOSTICISM

I often tell people I am a transgender woman. But what am I really? Proposed candidates include:

* Transgender woman

* Woman

* Sub-type of male

* Sub-type of female

* Unspecified third gender.

Mainstream trans ideology insists I am a "real woman," no ifs, ands, or buts. Gender critical radical feminists (also known as "TERFs") insist I am really just an effeminate male who lives and looks like a woman in appearance only (though many of them would probably insist no trans woman could actually "look" like a woman, which is bullshit, of course, and denies the lived experience of many trans women who are deep stealth).

Am I a unique kind of male or a unique kind of female? There is a strong intuition at work here that there is an objective answer as to what I "really" am. But in this essay, I want to resist this notion of objectivity as applied to gender identity. I agree with Preciado's statement "There is no empirical truth to male or female gender beyond an assemblage of normative culture fictions."[6] Moreover, even if there was an objective answer as to what I really am, I doubt we are capable of knowing one way or another. Hence, I want to propose and defend a kind of gender agnosticism. Gender agnosticism is the refusal to claim certainty that I know what my "true sex" or "true gender" is. Gender agnosticism is a refusal to endorse the sex/gender distinction and it is a refusal to endorse the elimination of the sex/gender distinction.

Bascally, gender agnosticism is about rejecting the need to have metaphysical certainty about the gender/sex of my body.

I don't know what I am. And it does not matter.

But what I do know are my desires. I desire to keep taking hormone replacement therapy because I have certain desires about how I want my body to look and feel, desires which connect with my desire to be seen in society a certain way. I desire to keep using my legally changed name along with she/her pronouns. I have a strong desire to wear clothes that can often be found in the "women's section" (ignoring for now the philosophical problems in trying to define what exactly "women's clothing" is—needless to say there are a few common themes in women's clothing).

I desire to walk into the women's restroom without causing a stir. I desire to walk into a room and not immediately have all the young children gawk at me for sticking out with my gendered presentation. I desire for my voice not to mean I am clocked as being assigned male at birth. I also have desires relating to my body parts that only certain surgical procedures can help satisfy.

I have no doubt about these desires. My internal knowledge that these are indeed my deepest desires seems secure.

So why do I need to claim knowledge about my "gender identity?" I refuse to play verbal games. There is not an objective test for gender identity in the same way there are tests for measles. And lest we think biology will give me answers, there is no consensus on how to define "biological sex." Most people think there are only two sexes: male and female. But Anne Fausto-Sterling[7] makes a convincing case that if we think deeply about intersex people, there are actually five different biological sexes, maybe more. Who knows. Two sexes? Five? Ten? It all depends on the assumptions we bring to the table. But at this point it does not seem to be a matter of simply doing more science and then we will figure out how many sexes there are, or even how to define what it means to be "male," "female," or something else. When thinking about sex and gender, value systems are never far away. The quest for objectivity is perhaps a pipedream. We need to embrace gender agnosticism.

I do not need to ground my identity in objectivity. I don't need an identity at all when it comes to gender. I am just me, a person with a unique set of beliefs, desires, and values. If I am going to identify with anything, it might as well be "philosopher"—after all, I find that tends to be the most predictive of my future behavior.

With that said, I want to acknowledge that many trans people take solace in gender gnosticism, the certainty they feel in knowing their own gender. They feel a deep psychological need to know they really are the gender they claim to be. Their identity is grounded in gender gnosticism. I don't mean to take that comfort away from people. Nor do I wish to argue that other trans people *cannot* have actual knowledge of their gender. Maybe they do. My bigger goal in this essay is to argue for gender agnosticism with respect to *my* gender and I hope to convince some of you of the epistemic and psychological merits of gender agnosticism.

Gender critical folks will continue to see trans women as men no matter how loudly we insist we are real women. Why? Because it's a debate about values not science. This is not a scientific debate or a controversy that will be resolved through clever experimentation. There is no smoking gun. There is no litmus test. There are just opinions, values, and desires. Ultimately, the debate about what we "are" as trans people is one of competing ideology. Do we want an ideology grounded in rigid biological conservatism, or do we want an ideology that gives us the freedom to self-identify as we please?

Regardless, why not try embracing gender agnosticism and see where it takes us? Let's base trans rights on ethics, not scientific certainty of our biologically grounded identity. Trans people do not need to prove we are "born this way" to justify non-discrimination legislation. We don't need a chapter written in a biology textbook to feel justified in wanting to have basic rights in this society. All we need to do is stand up as autonomous persons who demand that our personhood and core dignity are respected. We don't need facts about biology to claim our right to exist as free and equal citizens.

What we need are facts about violence, suicide, housing and job discrimination, and the satisfaction rates of hormones and surgery. We need facts about how to maximize the happiness of all trans people. We need knowledge about how to survive, not knowledge of whether our chromosomes are "really" those of a male or female. I don't need to know whether my brain is "female" or "male" to know that I want to be respected as an autonomous person capable of making my own healthcare decisions.

I don't know what I am. And it does not matter.

33

THE PROMISE AND FAILURE OF GENDER NIHILISM

> The gender nihilist, the gender abolitionist, looks at the system of gender itself and see's [sic] the violence at its core. We say no to a positive embrace of gender. We want to see it gone.
>
> *Alyson Escalante,* Gender Nihilism: An Anti-Manifesto[8]

Gender nihilism seeks to negate gender and the gender system in its entirety. Gender nihilism wants to see gender destroyed and nullified. Gender nihilism fails to see any net benefit of engaging and affirming the gender system—it is corrupt to its core and needs to go. Inherent to the gender system is the impossible task of living up to its expectations—failure to comply means violent enforcement and suffering. As the nihilist sees it, there can be no good from continuing to regulate all parameters of society through the lens of gender. A future without pain is a future without gender.

But is this actually possible? Is it possible to live in a world without gender? Gender nihilism on its face seems too good to be true. Just get rid of gender? Sure! What good did it ever do us anyway? But behind that promise comes the possibility of failure: perhaps it is impossible to get rid of gender. Perhaps it is like the multi-headed Hydra—you chop off one head and two more grow in its place. Perhaps then our attempt to kill gender will only make it stronger, but we will have deluded ourselves into thinking we have escaped it.

Gender nihilism argues that there is no gendered subject, no metaphysical "core" self to which our gender identity "rings true." Because there is no essential gendered subject, the nihilist sees any attempt to reify gender into a metaphysical truth as a form of violence against the gender and sexual minorities of the world, especially persons of color who have had colonial impositions of gender foisted on them.

Already we can sense a tension. Because for some trans people gender can be very affirmative, immersion in the gender system can bring euphoria, a sense that everything is finally "ok." So how can the reification of gender identity be at its core violent when some trans people themselves engage in their own personal process of reification? Can the violence at work operate despite the existence of euphoria? For gender nihilism to work, it needs to account for both the positive phenomenology of trans affirmation and the violence against gender and sex minorities.

But what is gender anyway? For gender nihilists, gender is a system of signification that operates through political regulation of coded signs. But the very way in which gender nihilism views gender renders it impossible to banish. This raises the question of whether gender nihilism's goal of gender absolution is even conceptually coherent.

Gender works through difference, feeds on difference, so as long as there is difference between people, then gender will work to codify and regulate those differences into a system of norms, rules, scripts, institutions, signs, hierarchies, punishments, and rewards. Gender nihilists insists that gender is a social construction, one they seek to see deconstructed entirely. But deconstruction never exists in a vacuum—there is always the corresponding constructive component working inside all human minds. As soon as we begin the process of deconstructing gender our unconscious minds will begin constructing it anew.

We are social creatures to our core—social interaction within a milieu of semiotics structures the development of the mind–brain system even from within the womb. Sociality is part of the essential structure of the formation of human minds. Trying to deconstruct the process of regulating social difference is like trying to deconstruct how we eat food: sure, it might be problematic in all sorts of ways, but we're going to keep on doing it because we have no choice, we must eat.

This illustrates a tension within the heart of gender nihilism—its insistence on anti-essentialism blinds it to the essential social nature of human experience. In other words, it is essential to normal human development to be raised in a culture of signs, a culture that works to take differences and turn them into constructed reality. If we apply anti-essentialism too enthusiastically, we risk losing sight of the bigger patterns that run through human life. And while these patterns could themselves change, my hypothesis is that the regulation of difference through semiotic coding is a feature of humanity that is here to stay, and likely only to get stronger as digital media landscapes have proliferated difference to a degree previously unimaginable.

Gender nihilism asserts that there is no substance to gender, that gender rests on a fundamental lie—that gender difference is constructed on a firm foundation. However, masculinity and femininity are constructed realities of coded significations that operate on the individual differences between persons. But can we group together differences into broad categories or not?

From a statistical perspective, we could choose to break the human species into two large camps. One camp is almost always assigned male at birth (AMAB) on the basis of a phenotype correlated with testosterone dominance and producing small, mobile gametes. The other camp is assigned female at birth (AFAB), with a phenotype correlated with estrogen dominance and producing large, immobile gametes.

That it's possible to break humans into two camps (with many exceptions, of course) is a product of evolutionary history. Sex, itself a biological phenomenon, has not always existed. Once created, however, it reinforced a dimorphism between small gamete producers and large gamete producers, the physiological essence of real, non-constructed biological difference. Biological differences that are not neutral mutations lead to real differences that manifest in different behaviors, thoughts, perceptions, desires, motivations, and physiological properties. These biological differences operate along a diverse and variable sexual spectrum.

Although it is possible to divide humanity into two distinct camps, it is never wise to ignore the alternative perspective: which is to view humanity in terms of the radical spectrum of individual differences that make us each unique beings. In this view, the intermediates, the edge cases, the outliers, all of our individual differences, work to make sex itself a polymorphous kaleidoscope. On this account, intersex and trans people might be *statistical* minorities but they are not *normative* minorities.

In other words, we can't necessarily read off how things "should be" from how things are, and just because intersex/trans is less common statistically doesn't make it "wrong" per se. Anomalous does not necessarily mean pathological. Accordingly, just because it's *possible* to lump most of us into one of two camps doesn't mean we *should*. Perhaps we can get greater scientific precision in our theories through a vision of sex as a spectrum instead of a binary. And in fact, many scientists are starting to think of sex, especially "neurological sex," in terms of a mosaic and not a strict binary.

These two views are complementary. Appreciation of evolutionary history compels us to see sexual dimorphism as a biological reality that works to create difference between males, females, and those who fall outside the strict binary. People and animals who give birth have different behaviors from people and animals who do not. This difference has existed for millions of years. At the same time, the radical individuality of human beings suggests that biological difference operates along a spectrum or continuum of traits. Appreciation of individuality helps us realize that the differences within the group of males is larger than the difference between males and females, and the same is true for females.

Individuality trumps sexual dimorphism but sexual dimorphism does indeed generate real difference. There is no such thing as a strictly "male" brain or a strictly "female" brain—all brains are a mixture of male and female structures, with more overlap than difference. But statistically there is a difference between male and female brains, though it is unclear whether the difference paints a clear causal pathway to the gendered differences between men and women. The intersection of nature and nurture makes it impossible to clearly delineate the contribution of biology to the types of high-level behaviors we see in human reality, for example everything that goes into being a scientist, or politician, or teacher, or any other profession that falls along gender stereotypes.

Gender nihilism attempts to collapse entirely into individualism without realizing that tremendous forces are operating to construct a dimorphic difference between male and female realities. Gender essentialism, in contrast, fails to grasp how sexual dimorphism is not biological destiny. People assigned male at birth are not imprisoned by this biological cage—technologies of gender now allow people to modify their biological sex through hormonal and surgical techniques. Hormonal technologies have also allowed for sex to be decoupled from reproduction through birth control. The pill has ushered in a new age of bioengineering. Trans people are also riding this wave of biohacking, being able to escape the confines of their assigned sex and transform the fundamental building blocks of their physiology through hormonal replacement.

Gender nihilism is a half-truth. But it is not a complete theory. Its goal of living in a world without gender cannot be reconciled with its own proclamation of what gender is. If gender is a system of signs that operate on difference, then gender will never go away because differences will never go away—variation is built into the heart of the evolutionary process. The only consolation the gender nihilist might have is that the strict gender binary might loosen its dependence on sexual dimorphism and be expanded into a multidimensional system of variables that arises from human biocultural individuality.

Gender itself is not going away but that doesn't mean gender is a static phenomenon, destined never to change. It's just about impossible to predict what the human gender system will look like a million years from now. But I guarantee it will be radically different, especially as systems of gender technology become more pervasive as social mechanisms of personal change. As technology loosens the grip of evolution on our sexed bodies, gender itself will expand to represent the infinite individuality of human variability.

Variation has always existed in nature. Variation is the essential building block of evolutionary change. And when you then add in the infinite variability of human culture, you take a variable system and exponentially increase its potential for variability. This is where gender nihilism gets it right. Gender dimorphic binary could in theory die off and be replaced by a system of gender that is multidimensional.

But gender itself is not going away. We cannot escape it. Nor should we necessarily want to. The violence inherent in the gender system is the same violence that drives evolutionary change. It is an inescapable part of the human experience. Of course, we can work to reduce the worst examples of violence, especially the violence of white supremacist, hetero cis-patriarchy. But the violent oppression of patriarchy is not the same as the creative violence of evolutionary change that works to create healthy variability in a population.

34

SEX CHANGES

Can anyone change their sex? In the trans community it's passé to call bottom surgery a "sex change operation." Many trans people believe they have always been their sex/gender and bottom surgery is merely bringing the body into alignment with the sex/gender that they have always been. In this way, they are merely bringing their body into alignment with their gender, which is why it's now often called "gender confirmation surgery."

Some people would argue it's impossible to change one's sex—sex is immutable from birth and whatever you were born with, that's it, you're stuck with it. They might say, "If you are born a male you will always remain a male." This argument is often used to invalidate the identities of trans people, regardless of whether one thinks sex is different from gender—the end result is that trans people are made to feel backed into an ideological corner.

In this essay, I will argue it is not only possible but relatively straightforward to change one's sex.

First, we need to recognize that most definitions of sex are stipulative in nature. Second, we should recognize that experts in the field often talk about many different "kinds" of sex, such as genetic sex, morphological sex, endocrinological sex, genital sex, reproductive sex, social sex, psychological sex. The exact number of different sex concepts usually changes from person to person. The key point of the argument is that when we are talking about sex, we are usually introducing some kind of stipulative component—"What I mean by sex is…"

So when we ask if trans people can change their sex we have to first decide which definition of sex we are talking about. (Disclaimer: this discussion is best framed in terms of a continuous spectrum, not mutually exclusive binaries of either strictly "male" or strictly "female" (c.f. intersex people).)

Genetic sex: trans people cannot change their genetic sex using existing technology. It's an open question as to whether scientific developments in the future will allow trans people to change their underlying genetic profile. It certainly seems possible in a science fiction sort of way and it would be rash to rule out this possibility given the rapid advances in the biological sciences, especially with regard to genetic manipulation with techniques like the genome-editing tool known as CRISPR.

Morphological sex: this refers to the "shape" of one's body. Trans people can change the configuration of their bodies with surgery, hormones, laser and electrolysis treatment, developing or removing the secondary sex characteristics that are often used to assign gender such as breasts, beards, body hair, skin texture, musculature, and fat distributions in the face and body. Some aspects of morphology cannot currently be changed, such as skeletal frame.

Endocrinological sex: your endocrinological sex depends on what the dominant sex hormone in your body is. If you are running on estrogen (E), you would be endocrinologically female; if running on testosterone (T), you would be male. Most people are running on primarily either E or T but men and women usually have some amount of both in their body. Women tend to have 6–86 ng/dl of T and anywhere from 100–400 pg/ml of E, while men tend to have 270–1100 ng/dl of T and 15–60 pg/ml of E. It is very unhealthy to be low on either T or E. You essentially have to choose whether to run on E or T for the rest of your life. Many trans people decide to change their endocrinological sex, and modern medicine is fully capable of enabling this transformation with HRT. The results are fairly remarkable.

Sex hormones are extremely powerful and change the fundamental operation of many biochemical systems in the body, leading to changes in morphology, cellular function, behavior, cognitive function, and emotion, to name but a few. Arguably, sex hormones are responsible for most of the perceived sexual dimorphism both in the animal world and among humans. The female spotted hyena is one of the few female species that is larger and more behaviorally dominant than the males, with an enlarged clitorus that resembles the male anatomy. It was hypothesized that these female hyenas had high levels of circulating T and this was confirmed when testing became possible. Thus, in some species, T is responsible for determining many sex-typed behaviors and morphological features such as body size and behavior. One could argue that while these female hyenas have a female genetic sex, they have a male endocrinological sex, social sex, and morphological sex.

Genital sex: trans people can change the configuration of their genitals with modern surgery and thus change their genital sex. This is the classic "sex change operation" or sexual reassignment surgery though it now goes by various other names such as gender confirmation surgery and gender reassignment surgery. One might argue, however, that contemporary surgical techniques do not change, for example, a penis into a vagina but rather create a new shape for the original set. But I prefer to take a functional approach: if you sharpened a stone enough it would "transform" into a knife because a knife is defined in terms of its use—a knife is something that cuts.

Reproductive sex: biologists sometimes define reproductive sex in terms of gamete size and mobility. Males are those with small, relatively mobile gametes (sperm) and females are those with large, relatively immobile gametes (eggs). With existing technology, trans people cannot change their reproductive sex but it does not seem impossible.

Social sex: your social sex is basically the complex semiotic system of gender/sex assignment done by other people. Your social sex is the sex other people assign you—it's how you are treated, how you are perceived, which social circles you are included in. Are you "one of the guys" or "one of the girls?" One of the more interesting things about being trans and changing your social sex is learning that men talk to men and women talk to women differently from how men talk to women. There are things men will talk about only in the presence of other men and similarly for women. Trans people have the unique experience of witnessing both of these phenomena, and it generally gives us a good insight into the psychological world of men and women.

Psychological sex: a person's psychological sex is the sex/gender they believe/feel/intuit themselves to be. This is more commonly called one's "gender identity" but I think it goes way beyond "identity." Identity has the connotation of something "on the surface," the identity you present to the world. But it has deep roots in our psyche. I have noticed if you ask cis people if they "identify" with any gender, they will give it a thought, and sometimes say, "No, not really," which is usually just another way of saying, "I have taken my gender/sex for granted my entire life and never had to think about it that much." In contrast, trans people think about the nature of gender in society and their sexed bodies at much higher rates than cis people. It's almost omnipresent for some of us.

Whether one can change one's psychological sex is an interesting question. I could see the argument going both ways. Many trans people report that they have felt like their gender since they were very little, suggesting that their psychological sex has been constant for their whole life, cemented in early childhood much like the "critical window" of language learning. In my own case, it seems more accurate to say my psychological sex has changed since I started to transition. I didn't come to understand myself as having a female gender identity until early adulthood and my psychological disposition has changed considerably.

This is a common narrative. Furthermore, many people report that after years of hormone therapy they "feel like a completely different person." E and T have powerful effects on the brain and thus it would be highly implausible that your endocrinological sex had no effects on your psychological sex. If you are trans, HRT usually has a diagnostic component: if changing your balance of E or T leads to a consolidation of your psychological sex, then it's very good evidence you are "really" trans (I'm going to bracket all the complex stuff that arises when we challenge the coherency of the concept of "really trans").

Many transphobes want to insist that if a doctor thinks you are male or female at birth, then you will always be the sex that the doctor assigns to you. This idea is used to create sex-segregated facilities that keep trans people out of the facilities that best match their gender, as well as governmental administrations making it difficult or impossible for trans people to receive necessary governmental IDs that best match their gender. But if we break sex down, it seems much more plausible that trans people often do indeed change more things about themselves than they keep constant.

After almost three years of HRT, I myself feel quite different from the person I was when I was running on T. A big difference is my emotionality and empathy. I don't want to imply that I am now a weepy, emotional, moody mess all the time (not that there's anything wrong with that, of course) whereas before I was a cold, stoic stonewall. Not quite. For the most part during day-to-day life I feel about the same mood as I always have, it's just that my reactions to emotional extremes have a different flavor. The tears flow much more readily, almost as if my body opens a release valve that was for the most part plugged up for the first 28 years of my life. I cried more in the first six months of HRT than I did in the previous 15 years. I do not perceive this to be a bad thing. Strangely, it's psychologically pleasurable, both in that it feels good to release that emotional pressure but also, to be honest, in terms of the psychological confirmation that yes indeed the HRT is working and my brain is running on E now. I am sure that trans men feel the same about their brain running on T—many of them enjoy the psychological changes that come from changing your endocrinological sex and appreciate being less "sensitive" to emotional turmoil, especially in the workplace.

In my view, the overall "most valuable player" of the various different sex concepts is your endocrinological sex. Arguably, whether you are running on T or E is responsible for more sexual dimorphisms than any other sex concept. Your chromosomes actually do not do much to directly determine your overall biological make-up—the causal networks are more fractal. Circulating fetal sex hormones have a much more powerful causal effect on your embryological development than your genetic profile as there are surprisingly large numbers of AFABs (assigned female at birth) with XY chromones and many

AMABs (assigned male at birth) with XX chromosomes and many variations in-between, such as XXY. Furthermore, changing your endocrinological sex is arguably responsible for the most effective changes in morphological sex, which lead to changes in social sex: when trans men grow beards after being on T for years their social sex is accepted as male by almost everyone, and when trans women have been on E for years their physical appearance is often changed enough to make female gender assignment natural and intuitive for most people (though not always).

So can trans people change their sex? The answer is "it depends" and "probably yes."

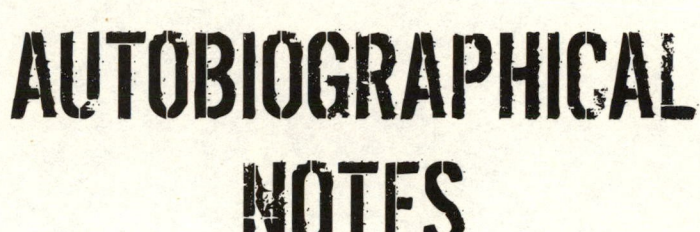

AUTOBIOGRAPHICAL NOTES

35

GIVING UP MY MALE PRIVILEGE

Before I get started, I need to make a disclaimer: this essay is entirely about *my* narrative. I not only want to speak just for myself but I believe I cannot do otherwise. Talking about trans women, male privilege, and male socialization is difficult because here, language matters. Words have power and the words "male" and "female" are not *strictly* scientific concepts—they are loaded with political, social, and personal connotations. When we choose to apply sex/gender terms to trans people without their consent we are are preventing them from creating their own narrative about their relationship to gender and directly causing pain.

With that, I can now get to the main point of this essay: I grew up with male privilege and then I began a process of giving it up. Already people don't listen to trans women: I've had people challenge this and say privilege is not just something one can "give up." But my experience tells me otherwise. My experience tells me that I'm now less safe walking down the street at night. My experience tells me that I should be afraid when I'm cat-called.

My childhood was remarkably normal despite growing up as a partly home-schooled evangelical Young Earth Creationist. As a child, I played Lego with my brother, built tree forts, played sports, rode bikes around the neighborhood, swam all day in the summer, played manhunt, collected random things, played video games, and was generally a pretty normal boy with stereotypical "boyish" predilections for sports, rough-and-tumble play, and so on. I also enjoyed secretly dressing up in whatever women's clothing I could find. My memories of the time are fuzzy. I don't remember if I ever had strong cross-gender identification at the time, but I did have daydreams of being treated like a girl. I don't recall ever being disgusted by my body, though, like many other trans people have expressed. That came later.

I am so very tempted to throw in the cliche "I never quite felt right" to summarize my childhood. In a way, it wouldn't be wrong. But I also think a lot of cis people also never quite felt right and continue to not feel right—indeed, not feeling right seems to be par for the course in modern civilization. I was not quite a social outcast. But I was a scrawny, bookish, goofy kid with a stutter. I had a select few friends growing up but was never the type to have large birthday parties with all my friends—I never had that many friends. Another cliche: I was a sensitive child. When I first came out to my mother she said she couldn't think of any "signs" of me being feminine as a child. I found this ironic because she had forgotten the time they grounded me for three weeks after catching me wearing her clothes. Threats of punishment gave me a very clear signal—I should be ashamed, this is not right for boys to do. So I buried everything deeply and went on like normal for as long as I could. I made it, surprisingly, to 28 years old before everything came welling up.

As a kid, I had a strong passion for school and academics. I always did well. I remember fondly competing with Jane Polkinghorn for academic gold stars in fifth grade. One of the most important "male" privileges I had and continue to enjoy is the privilege of never having my intellectual abilities questioned.

I had the privilege of never being discouraged to pursue science and philosophy. I had the privilege of never being defined as an "emotional being" but instead as a "rational being." I had the privilege of being seen as the "default"—the prototypical person.

Obviously as a queer trans woman I have lost my status as the "default" rational person; if anything, now my rationality is called into question as being jeopardized by my radical leftist trans activism and my political allegiance to the Social Justice Movement. But in my own mind I still think of myself as a rational agent in ways that are likely influenced by my male socialization. This privilege of assumed rationality was critical in enabling me to pursue academic philosophy, a field of inquiry that is dominated by people who pride themselves on their masculine sense of rationality.

I had the privilege of having my hand–eye coordination encouraged and praised. I had the privilege of having the option of not caring about my appearance without having my masculinity challenged. I had the privilege of not worrying about whether I was skinny enough to be attractive. I had the privilege of avoiding the "pink tax." I had the privilege of playing with all the "cool" toys as a child.

I had the privilege of being able to walk in my neighborhood at night without fear of being attacked or raped. I had the privilege of never having to worry about my drink being drugged at a party. I had the privilege of not worrying if I was getting too drunk.

I had the privilege to speak up in class and dominate class discussions. I had the privilege to go through grad school in philosophy without people assuming I wasn't "cut out" for philosophy, rational thought, or argumentation. I had the privilege of choosing any topic to study, even if it did not relate to the real world. I had the privilege to speak with authority and not have my intelligence questioned. I had the privilege of mansplaining.

I had the privilege of examples in thought experiments usually being male-gendered and I had the privilege of language being male-centered (e.g. "all of mankind," "all men are created equal," "mailman").

I had the privilege of not being interrupted as much when I was speaking.

I had the privilege of my reproductive system not being regulated by the state.

I had the privilege of my "male gaze" being the focus of pornography and I had the privilege of having my objectifications validated by society. I had the privilege of not ever being sexually harassed or hit on by strangers. I had the privilege of never being cat-called.

I had the privilege of reading about history and having almost every story center around men. I had the privilege of most of the protagonists in media being men with positive representation. I had the privilege of not having to deal with the Bechdel Test (google it).

I had the privilege of having almost all elected officials being men. I had the privilege of most research being done on male subjects.

I had the privilege of being able to take up as much space as I wanted.

I had the privilege of not having to worry too much about household chores and cleaning, so-called "women's work."

I had the privilege of everyone assuming that my career would take precedence in a relationship.

I have given all that up. I no longer have those privileges, or if I do retain some of the privilege, I am slowly losing it. I have lost my male privilege while also gaining the extra problems of transphobia and cis sexism. I have begun in earnest the process of unlearning all the problematic socialization I received growing up (while retaining aspects of "male psychology" that I still resonate with, such as my intellect). I have tried my best to learn more about feminism, women's rights, and the system of patriarchy that I used to benefit from. I try to be a better listener now. I try not interrupt people as much as I used to. I try not to talk over people like I used to. I try not to dominate discussions in class like I used to. Part of my newfound "quietism" is due to me not liking to use my voice and draw attention to myself as a trans woman, but it's also partly due to my recognition that I cannot take my privileges for granted anymore.

I recognize it is highly controversial in the trans community to talk about my having grown up with male privilege. I can only speak for myself. I cannot repeat that enough; it is not my place to talk about the experiences of other trans women, who might have had completely different childhoods that experienced their socialization totally differently. But it is unquestionable to me that I had certain privileges by virtue of being raised as a boy.

36

U-HAULING, RADICAL VULNERABILITY, AND THE EXISTENTIAL FEELS OF QUEER, POLY LOVE

Question: What did the lesbian bring on her second date?
Answer: A u-haul.

Queer women[1] are known for a phenomenon called "u-hauling" which is basically falling in love pretty much instantly and quickly setting in motion a complete entanglement, physically, financially, domestically, and emotionally.

In contrast, the stereotype for gay men is the tacit imposition to "not catch feels." So why do queer women fall in love so hard and practically sprint up the relationship escalator whereas queer men tend to engage in more casual poly networks (at least according to well-known stereotypes)? There are obviously exceptions to this rule, but even so we can ask: where did this stereotype come from? *Why* are queer women associated with rapid emotional intimacy?

I've been thinking about this a lot recently because not long ago I got out of a dramatic relationship where I was radically in love with a girl I had met three days earlier. And, of course, the feeling was reciprocated because she is also a very gay woman and while quite new to lesbian dating was falling right in line with every stereotype. I too am a living, breathing embodiment of this stereotype, especially since I had got out of a fairly serious relationship with a lesbian couple the *previous day*.

I am a big advocate of thinking that "coincidence" is an adequate explanation in more instances than commonly believed because the universe is often random and if you get enough people together in a room, someone is bound to flip a coin heads ten times in a row. A series of relationships strung together can be just as random as starting/stopping a relationship only a few times a year. Hence, I chalk up the rapid succession of relationships to cosmic coincidence, but how do I know I won't go on a dry spell in the future?

I have been toying with a tentative hypothesis to explain why queer women and not queer men have the stereotype of u-hauling. The story is something like this. Queer women are already on the margins of society both culturally and morally. While the tide is definitely turning, there is still so much hatred out there (in addition to lesser but equally frustrating types of bigotry)—it's almost palpable sometimes.

Queer women and anyone coded as a queer woman get harassed and violently assaulted or even murdered on a regular basis by virtue of being queer. This process of marginalization leads to a radical vulnerability.

But radical vulnerability is always half the equation for my speculative hypothesis about why lesbians are known to u-haul. The other variable is the style of communication common among women. In my experience, it typically involves deep honesty, sharing our vulnerabilities, trauma, insecurities, fears, but also our dreams and hopes as well as a healthy dose of laughter. There's a sense of solidarity that doesn't feel tribalistic.

As someone who has lived on both sides of the gender spectrum, it is undeniable to me that there is a communication style more commonly used by women and this style facilitates an openness that I think is hard for men steeped in machismo-culture to achieve. The "masc-for-masc" trend in cis gay male culture is indicative of the fact that gay men are men and, in my humble opinion, men and women tend to have very different communication styles.

For me, this is best encapsulated by how men and women sit with each other. When two men are hanging out they sit side-by-side facing forward, probably watching TV or playing a video game. Women, in contrast, are more likely to sit facing each other and engage in direct, face-to-face dialogue. But why is that? It would be naive to think hormones have nothing to do with it.

Most women are estrogen dominant, and, again, speaking from personal experience, the emotional valences work differently and work towards facilitating a more intense resolution of conflict. Those who have lived with both testosterone dominance and estrogen dominance often report that on T they are more numb. Whether that's a good or bad thing depends on the person. But for me, the lack of numbness has led to a softer and more empathic response to conflict that has fundamentally changed my communication style, especially in relationships.

And, of course, it's not just a one-directional causality for hormones. Reductive and overly simplistic models of behavior are just that, ideal models. But socialization and learning are definitely playing a role in shaping the gender gap in communication style. This is, of course, a classic chicken-and-egg question, just like the old nature vs nurture chestnut. As everyone knows, the answer is both unhelpful but also the only real truth—it is nature through nurture and nurture through nature. It is both. Interacting. In a very complex manner. Everything else is just details.

Having said that, I want to turn to another cultural stereotype within the lesbian community and that is the high emphasis on monogamy culture. By that I mean emphasizing things like soulmates, eternal love, the one and only, my everything, us vs the world, and so on. You can see monogamy culture working in the u-haul phenomenon because it is the sense that you suddenly have found your True Lesbian Lover who is going to satisfy all your needs until the day you die and you need to lock that shit down as fast as possible otherwise it could possibly fall through your hands and you'll die lonely and gay.

As someone who puts a high personal value on ethical non-monogamy, I am simultaneously drawn to monogamy culture and repulsed by it. I feel the temptation to use very possessive language and draw up mental entitlements to my partner's feelings, thoughts, and behavior. But my belief in something akin to relationship anarchy makes me naturally skeptical of formal hierarchy in relationships, including boundaries on what we allow ourselves to experience or not experience.

This is not to say I am against the idea of having a nesting partner(s). I am almost certainly someone who has a very strong nest-building instinct. But nesting is different from hierarchy and it is different from monogamy culture. Nesting is about mutually beneficial living arrangements but monogamy culture is about setting up toxic boundaries on our emotional openness.

And, of course, I am talking about monogamy culture and not two rational and consenting adults entering into a healthy monogamous relationship which is totally possible (but maybe for fewer people than one might assume based on the culture in which we live). Monogamy culture is toxic but monogamy itself doesn't have to be so long as there is still radical honesty, communication, vulnerability, and empathy.[2]

At the end of the day, u-hauling exists because queer women often spend their lives looking for something they didn't know existed until they have their first queer relationship. As someone who has dated straight women and queer women, there is a subtle difference by virtue of relating to the shared trauma of marginalization. That background serves to make genuine connection that much more cherished and leads to the rapid emotional escalation common to lesbians and bi/pan women.

37

"THAT'S SO CRAZY!"

Ableism, madness, and the politics of perfect language

Ableism is akin to racism and sexism but instead of skin color and sex it's about people with disabilities.

Ableist language devalues disabled people. A common example is when someone says "That's r*tarded," meaning "That's dumb" (which is considered another ableist term). This is widely considered to be problematic language by intersectional feminists.

But the language I want to discuss in this essay involves things like "That's crazy!" or "That's insane!" meaning "That's ridiculous!" The standard argument is that these terms, like the r-slur, serve to devalue and further stigmatize people with mental conditions like schizophrenia.

I haven't really talked about this publicly a whole lot but I have been diagnosed with various sub-types of schizophrenia over the years. I think the most recent diagnosis was something like "brief episodic psychosis." It's a long story I need to write up sometime, but needless to say, I am a certified "crazy person" and have a very real and personal connection to the concept of "insanity."

With that said, I personally have no problems with phrases like "That's crazy." To explain why, we need to dig down to the heart of metaphor.

Mental metaphors

There is good reason to think metaphor is at the heart of human cognition. Mental metaphors are especially important to everyday human life and the conversations we have with each other. We talk about ideas as objects and the mind as a container. Ideas can go "over" our heads, we can "hold" an idea "in" our mind, we can "turn" a memory over. The physical world of concrete action serves as a metaphorical landscape out of which we sculpt our thoughts about the world and how we communicate our inner life. George Lakoff and Mark Johnson are famous for elucidating how this works in books like *Philosophy in the Flesh: The Embodied Mind and its Challenge to Western Thought*.[3]

On the flipside, the mental life itself can serve as a powerful foundation for generating metaphors of its own. More specifically, I believe that metaphors surrounding normal/abnormal cognition function are integral to how we tend to think about the world. Phrases like "That's crazy" work so well to mean things like "ridiculous" because the possibility of our mind losing connection with reality is a well-known phenomenon and makes possible a sense of things being so fantastic as to be unreal, a ridiculous break from our expectations. "That touchdown was crazy!" "The ending to *Inception* was so insane."

When is "crazy" language problematic?

One of the ways things go wrong is when we use "crazy" to stereotype groups of people, for example "bitches be crazy," which is not only misogynistic but also ableist in so far as it's using "crazy" with a negative connotation as "irrationally emotional."

But how is this all that different from watching some stunt on YouTube and saying "woah, that flip was crazy!?" I think the latter is less problematic in that it is basically saying, "This stunt made me question my sense of reality," rather than the former, which is saying, "Women are irrational," which is not only false but actively harmful to a whole group of people who have historically been harmfully stereotyped as being too emotional to partake in the life of a citizen.

Another way "crazy" language goes wrong is when we use popularized conceptions of, for example, schizophrenia, to explain violent behavior, like when someone says, "I don't know why he shot all those people—he was just crazy!" In this example, they're not just saying, "The situation was ridiculous" or, "The situation violated my expectations of reality." Instead, they are saying the behavior can be explained by appealing to a condition like schizophrenia, a false explanation which is definitely harmful (people with schizophrenia are, in fact, more likely to be victims of violence).

Is it even possible to split the difference between "good" and "bad" usage of "crazy" language? Maybe we should just take the safe side and eradicate all usage of the term because if we're not sure of the possible harm, we should just not use the language at all.

But I think the quest for perfect language is difficult to achieve. To eradicate all ableism is difficult because so much of our language depends on unconscious body and action schemas involving "normal" human function.

Seeing is believing

Consider the schemas involving visual metaphors in the English language:

"I see what you mean."

"She is a visionary leader."

"Could you shed some light on that for me?"

The examples are endless. But all of these are arguably based on blindness metaphors in the same way that "crazy" language is based on metaphors involving disabilities involving psychic breaks with reality.

There is absolutely nothing wrong with wanting to educate people about ableism and remove problematic terms and phrases from our public vocabulary. The problem, however, is always going to be two-fold: defining the boundaries of acceptable use and running up against practical limits on removing "primary" metaphors from language.

Primary metaphors are the so-called "building blocks" of our cognitive life and are formed through our basic embodied interaction with the concrete world.

As it happens, being able to see is the statistically normal embodied interaction with the world and we can see this in our language and thought (no pun intended). That, of course, says nothing about the moral value of blind persons and their unique way of being-in-the-world. But in my opinion, trying to eradicate the "seeing = understanding" metaphor from our language is a completely Sisyphean task.

I think the same holds true of some aspects of "crazy" language, especially the connection between "ridiculous" and "crazy." What seems more tractable is things like saying, "That person is such a schizo."

But when someone says, "I am crazy about her" to mean, "The amount I love her is ridiculous," I personally am not bothered by it partly because I believe it would be futile to try to remove that powerful set of metaphors from our normal conception of reality.

The politics of perfect language

But here's the rub: maybe other people who have also been diagnosed with a "crazy" disease like schizophrenia do care. I never want to invalidate how other people feel about language use: although I am not bothered by some aspects of "crazy" language, maybe some people are and that's just that.

So this essay is not about giving able-bodied people license to just start using ableist language willy-nilly. I am not here to generalize a prescription for all language use. I don't believe I have that kind of moral authority. But what I am doing is trying to give an explanation of why I personally have not excised "crazy" from my vocabulary as a synonym for "ridiculous" in everyday language.

In the end, I believe the quest to make our language and thought more in line with our values should be about the ways we consciously speak and think about ability and disability. Often our unconscious minds are just jerks, usually brimming with implicit bias. Eradicating that is difficult—it's literally out of our conscious control. What we do have control of are our own conscious thoughts (that's why they're conscious!). And I believe it is these thoughts that serve best as grounds for assigning moral responsibility, especially in so far as our conscious beliefs inform the actions we take that may or may not actively harm others.

And, of course, I am against ableism just like I am against any other form of discrimination. But the quest to remove some metaphors from our language and thought faces steep hurdles. Of course, this is not an argument against trying it any more than the difficulty of eradicating racism is a reason to stop trying to eradicate it. But I think that the amount of mental effort allies take sniping at each other about removing metaphors from language could maybe be used more productively in engaging in educational efforts about the actual nature of what it's like living with mental illness.

I dunno. Like I said, I am not generally in the business of making sweeping normative claims of any kind. So I could totally be wrong about the utilitarian calculus involved in removing certain metaphors from our language. But I did want to open a dialogue on this topic.

38

QUEERING PERSONAL FINANCE

There is a tendency in queer/leftist circles to think that personal finance is for rich white conservatives and no one else. Wanting more money, financial security, retirement, investing in the stock market, and so on are not topics I ever hear any talk about in radical feminist spaces (except for discussing how problematic those things are). The generally accepted attitude is that capitalism is bad and that although it's ok to try and survive in that world, any attempt to *thrive* in the capitalist system is problematic because it inevitably exploits others.

But where to draw the line is difficult. For a radical queer/trans person to seek to get out of poverty seems to be ok. But to strive to be a millionaire? That is not a sufficiently anti-capitalistic goal. But surprisingly, becoming a millionaire through a lifetime of saving is realistically the only way to escape the capitalist system and retire. And do we really want to outlaw in feminist spaces the goal of retirement?

But part of what I want to talk about in this essay is how we can simultaneously critique the capitalist system that makes 401k-style retirement plans the only way to not literally work ourselves to death while also making it an extremely high priority goal in our own lives to work through that system and retire in accordance with the accepted financial wisdom (frugality, budgeting, saving, 401k plans…). Furthermore, I want to emphasize that marginalized people have an even greater need for sound personal finance than rich white conservatives precisely because they are marginalized.

When you are, for example, a trans woman working in the wage economy and trying to save up for surgery costs, it is a matter of grave importance to (1) live beneath your means (2) live frugally and (3) be diligent about saving. The medical costs associated with being trans are but one example of why having a keen interest in personal finance is crucial for marginalized folks. Far greater in importance is simply the concept of financial security. After all, if you cannot achieve security from society by fitting into the normative ideals of cis straight mono heteropatriarchy, it seems to be the obvious answer to gain security through self-insurance.

This is a particularly personal essay for me. Last year I filed for Chapter 7 bankruptcy. In a nutshell, I lived beyond my means in grad school under the assumption that I would eventually get that sweet, tenure-track job and quickly pay off my debts. That job never materialized and I was left with a large amount of consumer debt. During the bankruptcy, I had to live off cash and debit cards exclusively and that forced me to be more conscious of my finances. Out of necessity I learned to budget and developed a more frugal mindset. And budgeting is not just about writing a budget—that's the easy part—the hard part is following the budget, living up to the budget, adjusting the budget, and keeping that going, month after month.

Nassim Taleb wrote a book called *Antifragile*[4] about how true security is not about chasing after the positives but securing ourselves against the negative. In other words, we should strive to make ourselves less fragile. And not just that: we should strive to make ourselves *stronger* through perturbation. That is antifragile. Similarly, queer, marginalized folks' material security needs to be able to handle the booms and busts of the capitalist system otherwise it will be crushed. Easier said than done, of course. And, of course, we are assuming a lot about being able-bodied and privileged enough to grow up in the right environment for fostering the development of the neurological capacity for executive function, also known as "adult decision making." Not everyone is so lucky to be neurologically and physically capable to survive this system.

There is another intersectional worry with the admonition to be frugal and save as a means to escape the crushing reality of a capitalist system. A common refrain in personal finance circles is that spending $5 at Starbucks every day is counter-productive to the goals of getting out of debt and saving up for a downpayment on a house. However, the intersectional response is that when you are marginalized, the daily $5 latte at Starbucks becomes a release valve for dealing with society trying to beat you down for being marginalized. Furthermore, not everyone is capable of the self-discipline required for frugality.

But is this really the message we want to be sending to our fellow queers and marginalized folks? For me, it has the ring of a self-fulfilling prophecy. It says: we should not hold ourselves to the minimal standard of living beneath our means, which I believe is possible for almost everyone. And no, it's not about deprivation. Because we don't have to deprive ourselves of daily coffee—we just have to find smarter options, like investing in an at-home coffee-making product.

But will those $5 coffees really add up to anything significant? In a word, yes. Because it's not really about the coffee, it's about the attitude. It's about fostering the attitude of being a fierce saver of money. Our great-grandparents were forced to develop this attitude during the Great Depression so we know that masses of people are capable of adopting a frugal mindset as opposed to a consumerist mindset. After all, most leftists are critical of both capitalism as a large-scale organizing principle *and* all the micro-pressures in our society that encourage rampant consumerism fueled by aggressive advertisers.

There is often an assumption that the frugal lifestyle with its emphasis on budgeting is about deprivation but, in reality, it's about prioritization. What do we value? Do we value giving Christmas presents every holiday season? Then it's better to put a little away every month starting in January so we don't have to put the holidays on credit, essentially giving away our money to the creditors in interest. We obviously value our money otherwise we wouldn't work so hard for it. For every dollar we give to the banks for being in debt via interest, we could be giving to ourselves, securing our financial future. A budget is simply a written way to prioritize what we care about.

Saving for Christmas is just one example. Another example is prioritizing an emergency fund. If you drive a car, then you know that it will eventually need new tires, new brakes, and so on. That's a known fact. So saving up a small car-repair fund for that inevitability will save us from putting it on credit (thus avoiding interest and saving more money). This principle of having a fund of liquid cash to pay for random but predictable expenses is so important and highlights the need for saving.

An emergency fund of three to six months' living expenses is essentially the same thing. You never know when the next major crisis will happen, either a catastrophic car repair, ER visit, lost job, or inability to work because of sickness. Having an emergency fund to keep you afloat without going deep into debt or bankruptcy is critical for success. If you are debating going out to that brand-new restaurant but haven't saved up an emergency fund of $1000, you are essentially saying the risk of financial ruin is worth the latest chef's offerings. The frugal mindset is thus ultimately one that excels at weighing future reward with current pleasure.

But human psychology is stacked against us. Our brains are wired to focus on the immediate gratifications because from an evolutionary perspective we can't be confident we will be alive 30 years from now but the next 24 hours are critical to our reproductive success (which is what drives adaptive pressures to shape our brains to have the kinds of present biases we do that make it difficult to save for retirement). These kinds of rationality biases make it harder to do things we know are good for us (save money for the future) when we are tempted by things in the moment (spend money now for immediate pleasure).

So the deck is stacked against us. We are already on the margins of society, some with disabilities, and here I am asking us to just save more money and be frugal. If only you shopped at Costco and then you could retire! Seems laughable. But the seeming impossibility of seeing the final result (retirement) does not negate the *immediate* benefits of the frugal lifestyle. Frugality can add value at any time. It's never *not* going to be helpful because having control of our money is critical for peace of mind. So many millennials are intimately familiar with that horrible feeling of micro-stress lurking behind all financial insecurity. Not being able to sleep as soundly as we could because in the back of our minds we know we owe the bank $15,000. Or know that our car starter is likely to give out soon and we only have $35 in our checking account and rent is due next week.

In essence, I believe we need to be working towards queering personal finance. In queer/leftist circles, we need to normalize frugality, budgeting, retirement, and investing. Personal finance is not just for old white conservatives. It's for everybody. And it's especially important for folks on the margins because we cannot rely on society to provide us with security. Although society arguably *should* provide us with security for strong moral reasons, the fact is it doesn't. Not entirely. The safety net has so many holes and patches in it. Thinking about relying on your social security benefits to retire? That's not a risk I'm willing to take. Furthermore, the benefit would be so small (if it's still there in 30+ years) that you might as well start learning to be frugal now because you sure as hell will have to be frugal to survive on just the benefit alone if you haven't saved anything else up for retirement.

But am I assuming that marginalized folks don't have enough spare executive functioning to successfully engage in healthy personal finance behaviors? After all, there is a psychological cost to being on the margins. We might not have enough energy to make good financial decisions. I am fully sympathetic to this objection. But I want to make space for the possibility that many marginalized folks are likely to underestimate their own proclivity for smart financial behavior because it doesn't fit in with stereotypes they have internalized about what kinds of folks have smart financial behavior.

Furthermore, I believe we should continue to advocate for social safety nets and work towards democratic socialism. But in the meantime, us queers need to survive. It is either that or die. So in the end we have no choice—we must queer personal finance because otherwise we will inevitably fall through the cracks of normative society. To do otherwise is to let conservatives win the narrative about money: that money is something that only benefits old white people. Money can work for all of us. Indeed, we must as queers learn to have our money work for us.

Do you want to work every day until you drop dead? Neither do I. Logically then, we must as queers start thinking about retirement. That means getting serious about our personal finances. Because personal finance is, after all, personal. It involves the personal stake we all have in making our lives go better—and who doesn't want that? We all stand to benefit from queering personal finance.

39

T4T

I've been thinking about reappropriating t4t for a long time but my most recent relationship[5] stirred up these feelings again. t4t was a Craigslist hook-up forum (that FOSTA/SESTA killed) for crossdressers and trans folks to get it on with each other. Although it has a seedy connotation, I've been rethinking the potential of t4t as a framework for understanding trans liberation. Why should t4t be seedy? If we truly believe the meaning behind Laverne Cox's hashtag #transisbeautiful, then logically we should believe that t4t is beautiful. Moreover, I want to emphasis t4t is not naive separatism. It's ok to date cis people. But t4t is an attitude. A movement: by trans, for trans.[6]

I therefore propose we "depornify" and "desexualize" t4t.

There are so many possibilities surrounding t4t as symbol for trans liberation, an ideological sister to the old feminist politics of lesbian separatism but without the naive assumption we can all go off and live in communes. Instead of a politics centered on exclusion, t4t is about trans folks coming together to support each other.

All trans people invert the set of rules, norms, and expectations inherent to the gender binary—the binary system that says gender is immutable and fixed at birth based on superficial morphological features, the binary that leads to BS like the infamous "Free Speech Bus" that advertised the message, "Boys are boys...and always will be. Girls are girls...and always will be."

A c4c (cis for cis) relationship is so ingrained in our minds as being "normal" that t4t is harder to see as equally valid.

Decades ago, some medical professionals studying trans people developed measures for assessing the "success" of transition and the only relationship that counted as "successful" was being in a relationship with a cis person of the "opposite" sex. Any other relationship configuration and you literally lost points, your transition being deemed "less successful."

That's why t4t is political. It's inherently political even if we're not explicitly involved in activism.

People usually react to trans people being with other trans people almost with a sense of pity, as if that's the "best we can do:" settle for a fellow freak. People assume that our ultimate goal is to be with a cis person, to use their attraction to us as validation. I've been tempted before by the thought that if a cis lesbian is attracted to me, I must "really" be a woman! That sentiment is part of what makes t4t liberatory.

c4t relationships are ground zero for people coming to terms with their sexuality. Cis people, men and women, often unconsciously fetishize trans people for our bodies as well as "third-gender" us, being attracted to us as "exotic" or "interesting" but not quite accepting us at face value for who we are, or worse, having that attraction deflate post-orgasm, indicating the attraction itself was fundamentally objectifying and a product of horniness rather than genuine attraction. While it's ok to struggle with internalized transphobia (I do it every day), it's not ok to fail in our duty to interrogate our implicit biases and work to develop strategies that ensure these biases don't harm others.

So many of the narratives surrounding trans lives focus solely on our anguish, whether from our own dysphoria or from the marginalization we face at the hands of society, being seen as jokes suitable for throwaway comedy lines or memeification but rarely as full-blooded people with our own hierarchy of needs.

The personal is political

t4t is political because it aims to show how joyful trans lives can be away from the society that has such a hard time understanding us.

But, of course, we can never truly be away from society. The best we can do is form little nests and enclaves, little spheres of relative safety, places where we don't have to worry about being anybody but ourselves, places where we do not feel ourselves to be the 1 percent, the minority, the Other—places where we are "normal." Perhaps these spaces can only exist in fleeting moments and are never truly realized but my brain is able to take those disparate moments and stitch them together into a continuous memory and feeling, a feeling that is joyous and oriented towards the future.

For me, t4t represents a liberatory movement, focused on the advance of trans rights and our place within society. But the task of changing a deeply cis-normative society is so daunting, so overwhelming, that part of self-care is retreating into the solace of our own company, our own little queer/trans communities.

t4t is about solidarity. I want to make space to support trans lives, businesses, start-ups, relationships, artists, communes, spaces, political organizations, politicians, movements, and so on.

t4t is by trans, for trans.

It is community. But most importantly, it is love—love for ourselves, for our trans experience, for our existence—finding joy despite the pain, despite the hardship, feeling intensely those moments when we are truly affirmed in being ourselves.

While it is nice to have validation from the cis world, it almost always comes too late. The validation always comes after the lifelong internalization of transphobic messages we see constantly promulgated in the mainstream media, the numbing regularity of TERFism being splashed across op-ed pages and uttered by prominent feminists, the bullying and torment trans youth receive from their peers, the feelings of shame and guilt fostered by overly conservative parents, and so on. The messages are abundant and they are clear: choose to be openly trans at your own risk.

The strange loop of trans lesbians

I have dated, hooked-up with, and been in serious relationships with people of pretty much all genders: cis women, cis men, trans women, crossdressers, enbies, and trans men. I've dated several trans girls.

During this time, I've developed a theory about trans lesbian (transbian) relationships: they are strange loops, our sexual orientation endlessly flipping back and forth in transphobes' minds like the liar's paradox: gay, straight, gay again, now straight, gay, and so on.

The idea is that a true transphobe is going to think a "trans lesbian"—a trans woman into other women—is really just a deluded, "straight male." And straight males are into females, right? Well, the transphobe will also see my partner as a male, making us two "gay males," not two "straight males." But if we're not straight, then we must be into men. But we are now admittedly mostly into other women (with some exceptions).

So the transphobe can't make sense of our orientation without recognizing the validity of our gender.

Another thing I've thought a lot about is whether being with another trans person helps or amplifies dysphoria. In a very real way, it definitely helps. We don't have to worry that our partner isn't going to understand our dysphoria. We can vent about cis people, misgendering, anxiety, and so on without censure. My love for her body helps me love my own body. But precisely because our shared understanding has created a mutual vulnerability, I wonder if perhaps we enable ourselves to feel our dysphoria on a deeper, more intense level.

And I'm going to get real now: being in a relationship with a dysphoric person is not easy. Being dysphoric is not easy. It's like a tiny little knife in your gut that you know won't ever go away unless you kill yourself. Which sounds dramatic. But it's really not. The suicide rates for trans people make one stop and question: is it really the dysphoria or the combination of dysphoria and a cruel, hostile, transphobic, and unforgiving world?

Yes, there are good cis people (#notallcispeople) out there. Good allies and good friends to the trans community. I know many of them personally. But cis normativity and the corresponding cis sexism that arise out of it are deep, institutional structures and systems in our society. It's not going to go away any time soon and despite all the progress there are significant numbers of people who are skeptical about very basic stuff, like believing we are who we say we are—that trans women are women, trans men are men, and non-binary people are real.

The pains of our experience are also what give the joys of t4t a brighter finish. When we can share our happiness together, standing side by side, it's easy to adopt a kind of "take on the world" attitude, more specifically "take on the cis world" attitude. And I recognize that an adversarial attitude is not necessarily conducive to political allyship, but it's a venting mechanism. It's a way of engaging in radical self-care. Sometimes I just don't have the energy to care about being the perfect exemplar of political bridge-building. Hating cis people for propagating the implicit biases that structure the institutional biases against us is not done out of malice—it's done in order to cope, to make peace with our existence.

And furthermore, it fits into the general rule-of-thumb: always punch up. If you're going to shit on a group of people for comedic, venting, healing purposes, it's always best to go after those with more privilege than you, those who sit in a higher place in the social hierarchy. This general principle of comedy works for pretty much all intersections of privilege. When in doubt as to whether a group has "more privilege" (which assumes this can be actually quantified), it's probably best practice to just go "higher" until you find a group that clearly has boatloads more privilege than you.

Living as half a percentage point

Most estimates put the prevalence of trans people around 0.5–1 percent of the population.

Half a percentage point. You just kind of get used to being the only trans person in a room after a while. Tokenization is the inevitable outcome of being such a small minority. In effect, you become known as the resident expert on all things LGBT+. And, in reality, you probably are the expert. But you're likely to be the expert on other things as well. But you become known as the "tranny expert," the person to be consulted any time they see a gay person on TV or anything else loosely connecting to your own experience. Tokenization happens when someone randomly tells me how much they "love *RuPaul's Drag Race!*" as if I should, as a trans woman, be intrinsically connected to the experience of drag queens.

But I think besides the tokenization, the most impactful aspect of being an extreme statistical minority is the overwhelming sense of isolation I sometimes feel in the cis world. And that right there gives t4t relationships a special significance for me. I just feel less lonely in a deep, existential sense. I think it's why trans/queer people often surround themselves with other trans/queer people: it's a coping mechanism for being on the fringes of society. And the fringe itself is just not just economic or social, it's a philosophical fringe—it's being on the margins of intelligibility.

Despite being on the fringes of society, it's not as if I am not in society. I am in society. I am writing this in my house, which sits in the middle of a city. I go to work every day. I go to the grocery store, drink coffee at the local Starbucks. How could I not be in society? Yet I am outside it. Half a percentage point. It's kind of unsettling walking around sometimes knowing that there is a large percentage of people around me who would probably think I am delusional for just existing the way I want to exist.

In the end, t4t is political because the micro-personal is the macro-political. When trans people flourish in their relationships with other trans people, the very existence of our happiness stands in opposition to the implicit assumption of a cis-sexist society that trans identity is inferior and cannot possibly live up to the full-fledged moral-political life of cis identity.

t4t rejects all this and puts forward a radically positive message: #transisbeautiful.

40

LEARNING TO LOVE MYSELF

Sometime in the 1980s, Ray Blanchard wondered why some trans women pursue medical transition and others do not. Seeing trans women as an "interesting" research subject and something to stake a career on, he developed a grand theory or typology to sort all trans women into one of two mutually exclusive classes. Keep in mind there are roughly 30 million trans women around the world, all of whom—typical of humans—are unique in their particular combination of traits, quirks, personality, and dispositions. Blanchard nevertheless persisted, believing there was a pattern in the hodgepodge of data collected about trans women by gender clinics.

Central to Blanchard's typology is a term he coined "autogynephilia."[7] It literally means "love of oneself as a woman." Blanchard originally conceived of autogynephilia as a sexual fetish or paraphilia but recent formulations by Anne Lawrence frame it as a sexual orientation towards an idealized image of oneself as a woman. Basically, if you have autogynephilia, you get really excited by the thought of being a woman.

Either way, Blanchard became notorious for creating this typology. He claimed there are two distinct "types" of trans women with different underlying causes and clinical manifestations. The first condition is trans women exclusively attracted to men. The second condition is trans women who are either bisexual or attracted exclusively to women. Blanchard based his typology on survey data of trans women, which he had access to through the aforementioned gender clinics. According to his data, the first group was effeminate since early childhood and transitioned on average in their mid-20s. He said the second group was not effeminate in childhood and transitioned on average in their mid-30s. Furthermore, and central to his entire theory, Blanchard claimed that the two groups differed in terms of whether they experienced autogynephilia—erotic and romantic love towards the idea of yourself as a woman. It was not necessarily that the first group never experienced autogynephilia and the second group always did but rather that it was much more frequent in the second group.

The idea behind autogynephilia is that you love women so much that you want to be one yourself. You have committed what Blanchard called an "erotic target location error"—you have an erotic target (women) but you have located the target in yourself instead of in a "real-life" woman. Many trans women in Blanchard's second group reported that they could only climax by having an autogynephilic fantasy, imagining themselves to be feminized in some way or living a female gender role.

That's the theory in a nutshell. It boils down to the claim that there are two and only two essential kinds of trans women: those who are attracted exclusively to men and those who are attracted to more than one gender and/or just women.

There are many points of dispute for Blanchard's theory. It has been severely criticized along several dimensions, both theoretically and in questioning the data itself. I will raise only some of the possible worries about the theory.

Points of dispute

Sexual orientation as fundamental typology

There is no denying that there are indeed straight trans women and gay trans women. And perhaps they are different on average in certain personality traits, characteristics, or life histories. But so what? The problem is making sexual orientation the *fundamental* typological categorization, the Ur-difference if you will. You could also typologize trans women into those who have extreme dysphoria and those who have mild dysphoria. You could typologize trans women into those who are tall and those who are short. The point is that there are many ways to carve up a complicated biosocial phenomenon and it's not clear that sexual orientation is the most fundamental of all typological distinctions among the group of self-identified trans women.

Significance and explanation of outliers

In Blanchard's data, it's been pointed out that some straight trans women have autogynephilic fantasies and some gay trans women have very few if any autogynephilic fantasies. Blanchard argues that the best explanation for the outliers is that this effect is due to misreporting. He claims some straight trans women are "really" gay and some gay trans women are distorting their own history. Or could it just be that autogynephilia is experienced by both straight and gay trans women to varying degrees? Or that the whole idea is not a valid theoretical construct? This is only a theoretical "problem" if we are trying to hold on to our grand typological division into straight (non-autogynephilic) trans women and gay (autogynephilic) trans women. But once we let go of the quest to divide a complex multi-faceted group of people into two neat and tidy little boxes we no longer need to explain away massive discrepancies in the data and we can take the data at face value: things are messy.

Autogynephilic fantasies in cis women

It turns out that when you take Blanchard's survey scales and give them to cis women, many cis women also have autogynephilic propensities. But is the nature of the fantasy exactly the same as a pre-everything trans woman? Probably not. Cis women are not having a fantasy whereby their bodies are transformed. Cis women are (presumably) not being extremely sexually aroused by, say, shaving their legs or putting on makeup.

So even if cis women do enjoy the thought of themselves as women, the nature of the fantasy is probably not the same as that of many trans women. However, I do want to acknowledge the possibility that many trans women further into their transition may well have some degree of overlap in their fantasy life when compared with cis women. It's just more likely that for pre-everything trans women, the fantasies are not going to be the same.

Cessation of autogynephilic eroticism

It has been observed that the trans women who have a history of crossdressing fetishism or autogynephilic fantasies will often eventually lose the erotic component to their dressing or cross-gender fantasy and it becomes simply about doing what's most comfortable and makes you happy and/or what allows you to just live a normal life as a normal woman. Putting on women's clothing or wearing makeup no longer becomes arousing but instead becomes part of a mundane, daily life. This can happen pre-HRT, especially as trans women mature in their 20s and 30s, but it also frequently happens once trans women begin testosterone blockers and their libido diminishes, altogether losing the erotic component of their crossdressing and cross-gender fantasy life. At this point, many trans women decide to start working towards living full-time as women and they consolidate over time a stronger female identity.

Anne Lawrence, herself a trans woman often seen as a traitor by the community, proposes an analogy in order to rescue the autogynephilic theory despite the discrepancy in the data: this is the difference between puppy love and romantic love. When crossdressing loses its erotic component, Lawrence argues that we can still be autogynephilic and have a general all-consuming love affair and non-erotic fantasy life about being a woman, including having breasts and a vagina. It's just that the love becomes more about attachment love than it is about lust, but it's love nonetheless—love with the idea of yourself as a woman.

The problem with Lawrence's argument is that alternative hypotheses can be proposed that are equally compatible with the known data. It could be that the autogynephilic component dies off completely and is supplanted by a new psychological phenomenon that causes the actual start of pursuing medical transition through HRT and surgery. Saying that trans women with zero libido have gender surgery because they "love themselves as a woman" is not a very illuminating explanation because "love" in this usage is basically just a metaphor: not an operational concept of scientific precision. Saying trans women love the idea of themselves being a woman is more of a folk psychological explanation rather than a genuine explanation.

Clinical implications for medical transition

Supposing that the autogynephilic typology is valid, what are the clinical implications? Anne Lawrence doesn't think that autogynephilia should be a reason to not be eligible for HRT or gender confirmation surgery. Lawrence believes that medical transition can be a good option for trans women with autogynephilia. So it's not exactly clear what the purpose is of trying to divide your patients neatly into one of two categories if it doesn't change the eligibility criteria for HRT and surgery.

Need for universal theories of transgenderism

Despite all the grand theorizing of Blanchard and Lawrence, there remains a glaring hole in their entire theoretical apparatus: an explanation for why trans men and non-binary trans people pursue medical transition. They don't even bother to try to explain the phenomenon of trans men and non-binary medical transition. Why? I suspect it's because trans women are seen as more "peculiar" and thus more interesting as research subjects. It's also because if they attempted to find an explanation for why trans men and non-binary folks medically transition, they might realize a more universal explanation for why straight and gay trans women as well as all trans guys and non-binary folks medically transition. But they don't even want to investigate this possibility because they are too hung up on protecting the Grand Typology.

The naive quest for single factors

Another point of dispute is the idea of trying to find a single cause for why trans women medically transition. Proponents of autogynephilia theory want it to be the case that autogynephilic fantasies are the single cause of why gay trans women transition. But it seems unlikely for there to be a single cause for such a complex phenomenon, akin to the quest to find a single gene to explain a complex human behavior.

In my own experience, I transitioned for many reasons. I do have a history of crossdressing fetishism but to say that the *only* reason I decided to transition was because of that history is simply a naive and overly simplistic explanation. In reality, there was a confluence of multiple factors all pointing towards a certain transition pathway.

Terminology and respect

If you read the work of Blanchard and Lawrence, you might become really irritated by their choice of terminology. Blanchard calls straight trans women "homosexual" and gay trans women "non-homosexual" because he thinks of them as men and refers to their biological sex when classifying their sexual orientation.

Of course, trans people find this to be extremely disrespectful because if they want to even read this research, they have to deal with constantly being misgendered, which can be painful. I believe that proponents of autogynephilic theory should change their whole terminological strategy out of fundamental respect, as I have done so far in this essay. It's not that hard and it makes it possible for there to be more open dialogue between proponents and critics.

My personal narrative

Where do I fit into this story? I've spent three years coming to terms with my past as a crossdressing fetishist. I do loosely fit into the narrative Blanchard spins (I should note, of course, that Blanchard paints with a broad brush and thus captures difference through extreme generalization).

I was not overly effeminate as a young child—I enjoyed rough-and-tumble play, active sports, and playing with boys (I'm going to bracket a long and complex issue about what defines being effeminate and just use the standard definition), and I was attracted to girls like "normal" boys were.

But unlike "normal" boys, some of my earliest memories involved waking up to these quasi-lucid dreams of being forced to dress up as a girl as a punishment while secretly enjoying it, with a particular predilection for soft fabrics. I was and continue to be very particular about the texture of my clothing— utter softness is paramount (largely because scratchiness bothers me).

I would wear whatever scrap of women's clothing I could find and become aroused out of the sheer novelty and private nature of this drive. But was I having autogynephilic fantasies? Not really, though my memory is fuzzy (I don't fully trust my own memory that far back). I was not really imagining myself as being a female with a female body, female identity, living a life as a female. For me as a young child it was really more about the tactile sensations of the clothing, the hidden sense of the erotic, coinciding with my feminine dream life. It was not a fantasy of myself as being a cis woman as Blanchard described it. As I got into my 20s, the crossdressing did involve more autogynephilic idealization, especially as I took selfies of myself and attempted to be more "passable." But, of course, an alternative explanation, the one I prefer, is that this was repressed gender dysphoria expressing itself through my only possible alley of exploration: crossdressing.

In high school and college, I discovered trans porn. If I was having sexual fantasies at all back then, it was probably about trans women, not myself as a woman with a vagina living in a stereotypically female role. According to Lawrence's formulation, autogynephilia is becoming what we love—loving something so much we want to become the object of our desire.

The normal supposition is that what trans women love is cis women. But I was attracted to trans women (as well as cis women, and men, and pretty much folks of all stripes). So I want to coin a new term: autotransgynephilia—the love of oneself as a trans woman.

I eventually came to realize that the reason I was so fascinated by trans porn was that I was projecting myself into the bodies of the trans women as I watched and was deeply identifying with them. I realized over time that I wanted the body of a trans woman. I liked that aesthetic. I wanted that for myself, this particular mixture of the masculine and the feminine, like the ancient marble statue *Sleeping Hermaphroditus*.

I knew right away that I would always hate parts of my body. I also knew that changing my body would not be a long-term source of happiness so I would have to find a different source of meaning. I sensed that eventually my experience with my body would become mundane. I set in motion a long-term plan that is still unfolding, ever changing in small ways.

When I started transition I lost interest in looking at trans porn because looking at the larger-than-life figures only made me jealous and dysphoric. These girls had some alluring quality that was hard to pin down. Perhaps it was their feminine confidence despite the certain knowledge of their low status in society. It's funny how that works. I also grew to dislike the mainstream trans porn scene because of all the dehumanizing slurs, the fetishization and objectification, and how fake it all is. For example, the "cum shots" are not realistic—girls go off their testosterone blockers for weeks before the shoot to build up the money shot. These days I am more confident and can watch and even get off to trans porn as much as I enjoy any porn, which is rarely.

Suppose this story I just told about autotransgynephilia is valid. Would being autotransgynephilic delegitimize my identity as a trans woman? Or as a woman? Why? As I see it, gender is not just a social phenomenon. It is also a matter of self-creation. And why not create myself in the form I desire?

So what if I "wanted to be trans" or "loved the idea of being trans?" Is that really so bad? Being a man, or at least trying to be a man, was restrictive—as if I was locked in a cage of social expectations. I felt unable to do what I wanted, to look how I wanted. My "desire to be trans" is really just the other side of the coin of no longer wanting to live my life as I was: a crossdressing fetishist, hiding from everyone, ashamed, fearful, anxious, weak, lacking confidence. All the while I was living a dual life as a man, or at least playing the game. But I played the game pretty well, becoming a breadwinning, intellectual, respected PhD candidate in a wonderful hetero marriage on his way to the socially elite professiorate class, where I could go out to eat every week at fancy restaurants on the department's tab.

But I didn't want to play such a ridiculous game for the rest of my life. I had better things to do than waste my energy pretending to be this role just because that's what everyone predicted I would do. It just didn't seem as desirable as living a life as a trans woman, where the freedom to feminize myself (within the limits of what's possible and practical) could enable actual blending, to the point where I recognized myself fitting back into the cogs of the gender machine.

I do not mind sticking out *a little* but being coded as a flagrantly gender non-conforming male had no interest for me. More appealing was the possibility of being coded as a slightly masculine woman. I could always work on myself, slowly eliminate elements of the masculine I carried with me. I knew, however, that I would always carry more of the masculine with me than typical women. So I set out to create a paradox: to be effortlessly feminine yet have confidence in the strength that came from my history as an amateur bodybuilder and powerlifter.

Maybe I wanted to socially and medically transition because that would make me happier. Maybe I saw a chance to walk my own path. If so, what's wrong with that? So long as I do not hurt anyone else, why does it matter if I'd rather "choose" to be a trans woman and all it entails—good and bad—than choose to remain living my life where everyone thinks of me as a cis male? Is that so bad? Mainstream trans discourse is so hung up on bio-neurological explanations of I was "born this way," focusing on brain sex theories, fetal hormone levels, and so on.

None of that matters to me. I do not know whether I have a "male brain" or a "female brain"—I've never looked at my brain before. But I do know what will make me happy. I do know what my desires are and I know how to take steps to satisfy those desires. I know my desires are not causing anyone else any harm. I know I am happier on HRT than I was before HRT. I know how I want my body to look and I know how I don't want my body to look. I know how I want others to perceive me and treat me. Scientific technology is available to help me satisfy my desires and I plan on taking full advantage of that technology to help myself live a more enjoyable and satisfying life.

Is being a trans woman such a shitty thing to be in our society that no one in their right mind would rationally choose to be a trans woman? That doesn't make sense to me. It seems possible that someone could think they'd be happier as a trans woman than being a cis male not because they think they "are a woman" deep down in their brain but because social and medical transition would satisfy their unique set of desires formed by a unique combination of nature and nurture. That's me. I chose to be trans.

FURTHER RESOURCES

Trans feminism, gender studies, and bioethics

Baril, A. (2015) "Needing to acquire a physical impairment/disability: thinking the connections between trans and disability studies through transability." *Hypatia*, 30(1), 30–48.

Bettcher, T.M. (2006a) "Understanding Transphobia: Authenticity and Sexual Abuse." In K. Scott-Dixon (ed.) *Trans/forming Feminisms: Transfeminist Voices Speak Out*, pp.203–210. Toronto: Sumach Press.

Bettcher, T.M. (2006b) "Appearance, Reality, and Gender Deception: Reflections on Transphobic Violence and the Politics of Pretence." In F. Murchadha (ed.) *Violence, Victims, and Justifications*, pp.174–200. New York, NY: Peter Lang Press.

Bettcher, T.M. (2007) "Evil deceivers and make-believers: transphobic violence and the politics of illusion." *Hypatia*, 22(3), 43–65.

Butler, J. (1990) *Gender Trouble: Feminism and the Subversion of Identity*. New York, NY: Routledge.

Currah, P., Juang, R.M., and Minter, S.P. (eds.) (2006) *Transgender Rights*. Minneapolis, MN: University of Minnesota Press.

Draper, H. (1988) "Transsexualism and sex reassignment." *Journal of Medical Ethics*, 14(1), 47–48.

Feinberg, L. (1998) *Trans Liberation: Beyond Pink or Blue*. Boston, MA: Beacon Press.

Haraway, D.J. (1991) "A Cyborg Manifesto: Science, Technology, and Socialist-Feminism in the Late Twentieth Century." In *Simians, Cyborgs, and Women: The Reinvention of Nature*, pp.149–182. New York, NY: Routledge.

Lane, R. (2009) "Trans as bodily becoming: rethinking the biological as diversity, not dichotomy." *Hypatia*, 24(3), 136–157.

Mason, N. (1980) "The transsexual dilemma: being a transsexual." *Journal of Medical Ethics*, 6(2), 85–89.

Mckinnon, R. (2014) "Stereotype threat and attributional ambiguity for trans women." *Hypatia*, 29(1), 857–872.

Namaste, V. (2000) *Invisible Lives: The Erasure of Transsexual and Transgendered People*. Chicago: University of Chicago Press.

Namaste, V. (2005) *Sex Change, Social Change: Reflections on Identity, Institutions, and Imperialism*. Toronto: Canadian Scholars' Press.

Salamon, G. (2010) *Assuming a Body: Transgender and Rhetorics of Materiality*. New York, NY: Columbia University Press.

Scott-Dixon, K. (ed.) (2006) *Trans/forming Feminisms: Transfeminist Voices Speak Out*. Toronto: Sumach Press.

Scott-Dixon, K. (2009) "Public health, private parts: a feminist public-health approach to trans issues." *Hypatia*, 24(3), 33–55.

Serano, J. (2007) *Whipping Girl: A Transsexual Woman on Sexism and the Scapegoating of Femininity*. Berkeley, CA: Seal Press.

Serano, J. (2013) *Excluded: Making Feminist and Queer Movements More Inclusive*. Berkeley, CA: Seal Press.

Shrage, L. (2009) *You've Changed: Sex Reassignment and Personal Identity*. Oxford: Oxford University Press.

Snorton, C.R. (2009) "'A new hope': the psychic life of passing." *Hypatia*, 24(3), 77–92.

Stone, S. (2006) "The Empire Strikes Back: A Posttranssexual Manifesto." In S. Stryker and S. Whittle (eds) *The Transgender Studies Reader*, pp.221–235. New York, NY: Routledge.

Sycamore, M. (2007) *Nobody Passes: Rejecting the Rules of Gender and Conformity*. Berkeley, CA: Seal Press.

Towle, E.B. and Morgan, L.M (2006) "Romancing the Transgender Native: Rethinking the Use of the 'Third Gender' Concept." In S. Stryker and S. Whittle (eds) *The Transgender Studies Reader*, pp.666–684. New York, NY: Routledge.

Trans history

Benjamin, H. (1966) *The Transsexual Phenomenon*. New York, NY: Julian Press.

Bolin, A. (1988) *In Search of Eve*. Hadley, MA: Nergin & Garvey Publishers.

Califia, P. (1997) *Sex Changes: Transgender Politics*. San Francisco, CA: Cleis Press.

Feinberg, L. (1996) *Transgender Warriors: Making History from Joan of Arc to Dennis Rodman*. Boston, MA: Beacon Press.

Green, R. and Money, J. (eds) (1969) *Transsexualism and Sex Reassignment*. Baltimore, MD: The Johns Hopkins Press.

Hausman, B.E. (1995) *Changing Sex: Transsexualism, Technology, and the Idea of Gender*. Durham, NC: Duke University Press.

Hirshfeld, M. (1991) *Transvestites: The Erotic Drive to Cross-Dress* (translated by Michael A. Lombardi-Nash) Buffalo, NY: Prometheus Books.

Jorgensen, C. (1967) *Christine Jorgensen: A Personal Autobiography*. New York, NY: Paul Eriksson.

Meyerowitz, J. (2002) *How Sex Changed: A History of Transsexuality in the United States*. Cambridge, MA: Harvard University Press.

Meyerowitz, J. (2006) "A 'Fierce and Demanding' Drive." In S. Stryker and S. Whittle (eds) *The Transgender Studies Reader*, pp.362–386. New York, NY: Routledge.

[NOTE: highly transphobic] Raymond, J. (1979) *The Transsexual Empire: The Making of the She-Male*. Boston, MA: Beacon Press.

Reay, B. (2014) "The transsexual phenomenon: a counter-history." *Journal of Social History*, 47(4), 1042–1070.

Stryker, S. (2008) *Transgender History*. Berkeley, CA: Seal Press.

Thomson, J.M. (1980) "Transsexualism: a legal perspective." *Journal of Medical Ethics*, 6(2), 92–97.

Trans narratives

Conn, C. (1977) *Canary: The Story of a Transsexual*. New York, NY: Bantam Books.

Bornstein, K. (2012) *A Queer and Pleasant Danger: A Memoir*. New York, NY: Beacon Press.

Brevard, A. (2001) *Woman I Was Not Born to Be: A Transsexual Journey*. Philadelphia, PA: Temple University Press.

Morris, J. (1974) *Conundrum*. New York, NY: Harcourt Brace Jovanovich.

Scholinski, D. and Adams, J.M. (1997) *The Last Time I Wore a Dress*. New York, NY: Riverhead Books.

The science of gender

Aloisi, A.M., Bachiocco, V., Costantino, A., Stefani, R., *et al.* (1980) "Transsexualism: a medical perspective." *Journal of Medical Ethics*, 6(2), 90–91.

Bailey, J.M. and Triea, K. (2007) "What many transgender activists don't want you to know: and why you should know it anyway." *Perspectives in Biology and Medicine*, 50(4), 521–534.

Blanchard, R., Steiner, B.W., Clemmensen, L.H., and Dickey, R. (1989) "Prediction of regrets in postoperative transsexuals." *Canadian Journal of Psychiatry*, 34, 43–45.

Bucar, E.M. (2010) "Bodies at the margins: the case of transsexuality in Catholic and Shia ethics." *Journal of Religious Ethics*, 38(4), 601–615.

Cohen-Kettenis, P. (1999) "Transsexualism: a review of etiology diagnosis and treatment." *Journal of Psychosomatic Research*, 46(4), 315–333.

Cohen-Kettenis, P. and Van Goozen, S. (1997) "Sex reassignment of adolescent transsexuals: a follow-up study." *Journal of the American Academy of Child & Adolescent Psychiatry*, 36(2), 263–271.

De Cuypere, G., T' Sjoen, G., Beerten, R., Selvaggi, G., *et al.* (2005) "Sexual and physical health after sex reassignment surgery." *Archives of Sexual Behavior*, 34(6), 679–690.

Diamond, M. and Sigmundson, H.K. (1997) "Sex reassignment at birth: long-term review and clinical implications." *Archives of Pediatrics & Adolescent Medicine*, 151(3), 298–304.

Dittrich, R., Binder, H., Cupisti, S., Hoffmann, I., Beckmann, M.W., and Mueller, A. (2005) "Endocrine treatment of male-to-female transsexuals using gonadotropin-releasing hormone agonist." *Experimental and Clinical Endocrinology and Diabetes*, 113(10), 586–592.

Drescher, J. (2010) "Queer diagnoses: parallels and contrasts in the history of homosexuality, gender variance, and the Diagnostic and Statistical Manual." *Archives of Sexual Behavior*, 39(2), 427–460.

Edgerton, M.T., Knorr, N.J., and Callison, J.R. (1970) "The surgical treatment of transsexual patients. Limitations and indications." *Plastic and Reconstructive Surgery*, 45(1), 38.

Haas, A.P., Eliason, M., Mays, V.M., *et al.* (2011) "Suicide and suicide risk in lesbian, gay, bisexual, and transgender populations: review and recommendations." *Journal of Homosexuality*, 58(1), 10–51.

Hale, C.J. (2007) "Ethical problems with the mental health evaluation standards of care for adult gender variant prospective patients." *Perspectives in Biology and Medicine*, 50(4), 491–505.

Hare, L., Bernard, P., Sánchez, F.J., Baird, P.N., *et al.* (2009) "Androgen receptor repeat length polymorphism associated with male-to-female transsexualism." *Biological Psychiatry*, 65(1), 93–96.

Khoosal, D., Grover, P., and Terry, T. (2011) "Satisfaction with a gender realignment service." *Sexual and Relationship Therapy*, 26(1), 72–83.

Kockott, G. and Fahrner, E.M. (1987) "Transsexuals who have not undergone surgery: a follow-up study." *Archives of Sexual Behavior*, 16(6), 511–522.

Kruijver, F.P., Zhou, J.N., Pool, C.W., Hofman, M.A., Gooren, L.J., and Swaab, D.F. (2000) "Male-to-female transsexuals have female neuron numbers in a limbic nucleus." *The Journal of Clinical Endocrinology & Metabolism*, 85(5), 2034–2041.

Kuiper, A.J. and Cohen-Kettenis, P.T. (1998) "Gender role reversal among postoperative transsexuals." *International Journal of Transgenderism*, 2(3).

Landén, M., Wålinder, J., Hambert, G., and Lundström, B. (1998) "Factors predictive of regret in sex reassignment." *Acta Psychiatrica Scandinavica*, 97(4), 284–289.

Lawrence, A.A. (2003) "Factors associated with satisfaction or regret following male-to-female sex reassignment surgery." *Archives of Sexual Behavior*, 32(4), 299–315.

Levy, A., Crown, A., and Reid, R. (2003) "Endocrine intervention for transsexuals." *Clinical Endocrinology*, 59(4), 409–418.

Lindemalm, G., Korlin, D., and Uddenberg, N. (1986) "Long-term follow-up of 'sex change' in 13 male-to-female transsexuals." *Archives of Sexual Behavior*, 15, 187–210.

Lombardi, E.L., Wilchins, R.A., Priesing, D., and Malouf, D. (2002) "Gender violence: transgender experiences with violence and discrimination." *Journal of Homosexuality*, 42(1), 89–101.

Lothstein, M. (1982) "Sex reassignment surgery: historical, bioethical, and theoretical issues." *American Journal of Psychiatry*, 139(4), 417–426.

Luders, E., Sánchez, F.J., Gaser, C., Toga, A.W., *et al.* (2009) "Regional gray matter variation in male-to-female transsexualism." *Neuroimage*, 46(4), 904–907.

Marks, I., Green, R., and Mataix-Cols, D. (2000) "Adult gender identity disorder can remit." *Comprehensive Psychiatry*, 41, 273–277.

Meriggiola, M.C. (2007) "Cross-sex hormone administration changes pain in transsexual women and men." *Pain*, 132, S60–S67.

Meyer-Bahlburg, H.F. (2010) "From mental disorder to iatrogenic hypogonadism: dilemmas in conceptualizing gender identity variants as psychiatric conditions." *Archives of Sexual Behavior*, 39(2), 461–476.

Murad, M.H., Elamin, M.B., Garcia, M.Z., Mullan, R.J., *et al.* (2010) "Hormonal therapy and sex reassignment: a systematic review and meta-analysis of quality of life and psychosocial outcomes." *Clinical Endocrinology*, 72(2), 214–231.

Olsson, S.E. and Möller, A. (2006) "Regret after sex reassignment surgery in a male-to-female transsexual: a long-term follow-up." *Archives of Sexual Behavior*, 35(4), 501–506.

Ramachandran, V.S. (2008) "Phantom penises in transsexuals." *Journal of Consciousness Studies*, 15(1), 5–16.

Rametti, G., Carrillo, B., Gómez-Gil, E., Junque, C., *et al.* (2011) "White matter microstructure in female to male transsexuals before cross-sex hormonal treatment. A diffusion tensor imaging study." *Journal of Psychiatric Research*, 45(2), 199–204.

Safer, J. and Tangpricha, V. (2008) "Out of the shadows: it is time to mainstream treatment for transgender patients." *Endocrine Practice*, 14(2), 248–250.

Saraswat, A., Weinand, J.D., and Safer, J.D. (2015) "Evidence supporting the biologic nature of gender identity." *Endocrine Practice*, 21(2), 199–204.

Toorians, A.W., Thomassen, M.C., Zweegman, S., *et al.* (2003) "Venous thrombosis and changes of hemostatic variables during cross-sex hormone treatment in transsexual people." *Journal of Clinical Endocrinology and Metabolism*, 88, 5723–5729.

Van Kesteren, P., Megens, J.A.J., Asscheman, H., and Gooren, L.J.G. (1997) "Side effects of cross-sex hormone administration in transsexuals." *Clinical Endocrinology*, 47, 337.

Zhou, J.N., Hofman, M.A., Gooren, L.J., and Swaab, D.F. (1995) "A sex difference in the human brain and its relation to transsexuality." *Nature*, 378(6552), 68–70.

NOTES

Preface

1. www.transphilosopher.com.
2. "Trannies, traps, and the third gender," "Sapiosexualism is here to stay," "The inherent superiority of softness," "Nobody is trans enough," and "t4t."
3. This is a reference to one of my favorite books on writing of all time: Thomas, F.N. and Turner, M. (2011) *Clear and Simple as the Truth*. Princeton, NJ: Princeton University Press.

Transfeminine Blues

1. I'm currently undecided, leaning towards keeping it. Which does not mean I like it. I don't. I hate it. But I have my reasons for not wanting the surgery (yet).
2. When I first wrote this essay, US Congress hadn't passed the Stop Enabling Sex Traffickers Act (SESTA) and the Allow States and Victims to Fight Online Sex Trafficking Act (FOSTA), which recently killed the Craigslist personals sections, including the infamous m4t forum. The bills do much more than that, unfortunately, and if you listen to sex workers, they are saying that these bills—supposedly aimed at helping them—only work to harm them and further push them into the dangerous underground without any way to screen clients and set up safe channels of communication. Furthermore, the bills expand the prison–industrial complex by putting more bodies in prison while ignoring what actually needs to be done: legalization of consensual sex work between rational adults.

3. The irony of this assumption is that trans women's bodies are, in my experience, far more mysterious in terms of how they connect to sexual pleasure. This is largely due to having to navigate around dysphoria and a re-wired hormonal system.

4. Serano, J. (2007) *Whipping Girl: A Transsexual Woman on Sexism and the Scapegoating of Femininity*. Berkeley, CA: Seal Press.

5. This scenario will be slightly harder to play out now that FOSTA has been passed by Congress. However, sex workers themselves did not want FOSTA passed and are actively threatened by this legislation.

6. Valerio, M.W. (2006) *The Testosterone Files: My Hormonal and Social Transformation from Female to Male*. San Francisco, CA: Seal Press, p.6.

7. Bornstein, K. (1994) *Gender Outlaw: On Women, Men, and the Rest of Us*. New York, NY: Routledge, p.8.

8. Trans Exclusionary Radical Feminist. A common TERF tactic is to claim that "TERF" is a slur and then contact the employers of trans women and try to get them fired for using "misogynistic slurs against women." But "TERF" is not a slur in and of itself in the same way "f*ggot" and the n-word are. The f-word and the n-word are paradigmatic examples of slurs. There is *no way* to use those words without causing some kind of tacit harm. That's what makes them slurs: the long history of actual violence and discrimination enacted on marginalized people.

    But "TERF" is an acronym. None of the words it stands for is a slur because each word can be used in non-inflammatory sentences. The same cannot be said of "whore" and "f*g"—if these words remain in sentences the sentence becomes inflammatory by virtue of the decision to not use less inflammatory versions like "sex worker" or medical language like "vagina." Obviously, "trans" is not a slur. Nor is it a slur to call someone "exclusionary"—that is merely a description. It is also not a slur to call someone radical or to call them a feminist. They might disagree about being called those things but that doesn't make them a slur because slurs are generated by a history of oppression and there is no history of trans people oppressing these "gender critical" feminists—if anything, it is the opposite.

    They point out that trans people say things like "Kill out TERFs." But this is an example of "punching up" to your oppressors—a common venting method as a marginalized class. But to my knowledge, there is not a history of TERFs being bullied into suicide or violently murdered in the way trans women are on the basis of pervasive cis sexism.

    So when you break down the meaning of "TERF" it becomes possible to use the term "TERF" in a non-inflammatory manner to describe those people who identify as feminists with a "radical" bent who want to exclude trans women from the category of women and trans men from the category of men. Furthermore, the term "TERF" itself was coined not by trans people but by cis feminists. It was started as a neutral term. The same cannot be said of actual slurs like the f-word or the n-word.

9. "Ur" means earliest, original, denoting the the primal stage of a historical or cultural entity or phenomenon.

10. Preciado, P.B. (2013) *Testo Junkie: Sex, Drugs, and Biopolitics in the Pharmacopornographic Era*. New York, NY: The Feminist Press, p.236.

11. The Lockean model essentially states that personal identity is a matter of continuity between psychological states such as memory.

12. Bornstein, K. (1994) *Gender Outlaw: On Women, Men, and the Rest of Us*. New York, NY: Routledge, p.135.

13. See my essay in this collection: "The inherent superiority of softness."

14. Lorde, A. (1981) "The Uses of Anger: Women Responding to Racism." National Women's Studies Association Conference, Storrs, Connecticut. Accessed on 10/09/2018 at www.blackpast.org/1981-audre-lorde-uses-anger-women-responding-racism.

Feminist Musings

1. Lorde, A. (2012) *Sister Outsider: Essays and Speeches*. Berkeley, CA: Crossing Press, p.122.

2. "Stoked on sapiosexuality." Available at http://wolfieboy.livejournal.com/2262.html.

3. de Beauvoir, S. (1953) *The Second Sex* (translated by H.M Parshley). New York, NY: Alfred A. Knopf, p.330.

4. I must admit, the identity of "writer" is slowly creeping up on "philosopher" as the primary self-narrative. But I suspect that to the extent my identity as a writer becomes more dominant in my own self-understanding it will fuse with "philosopher" to become something akin to "writer of philosophical experience."

5. Brown, B. (2010) *The power of vulnerability*. Video recording, available at www.ted.com/talks/brene_brown_on_vulnerability?language=en.

6. Friedan, B. (2001, first published 1963) *The Feminine Mystique*. New York, NY: W.W. Norton.

7. de Kruif, P. (1945) *The Male Hormone*. New York, NY: Harcourt, Brace and Co.

8. Jorgensen quoted in Rudacille, D. (2005) *The Riddle of Gender*. New York, NY: Pantheon Books, p.75.

9. Jorgensen quoted in Rudacille, D. (2005) *The Riddle of Gender*. New York, NY: Pantheon Books, p.80.

10. Stone, S. (2006) "The Empire Strikes Back: A Posttranssexual Manifesto." In S. Stryker and S. Whittle (eds) *The Transgender Studies Reader*, pp.221–235. New York, NY: Routledge.

Life in Transition

1. A repeating motif of my pre-transition life was dreaming of excuses to shave my legs and "get away with it" as a man. I did a lot of googling. Some answers I toyed with: taking up road cycling (for preventing gravel getting into rashes, of course), swimming (to reduce resistance), bodybuilding (show off muscle definition), and the one I finally settled on: vanity (I just like how it looks/feels).

2. I can vouch for the idea, however, that there are things men only talk about in the company of men (or at least people they believe to be men).

3. I still get misgendered often enough, especially in the uniforms I've been wearing lately working in the food industry, which itself deserves its own essay. Let's just say I have been meditating lately on the gendered nature of the delivery service.

4. Bornstein, K. (2012) *A Queer and Pleasant Danger*. Boston, MA: Beacon Press, p.203.

5. Serano, J. (2007) *Whipping Girl: A Transsexual Woman on Sexism and the Scapegoating of Femininity*. Berkeley, CA: Seal Press.

6. I'm assuming certain things about the connection between conceptual vs metaphysical possibility, but this is my book so I don't really care if these assumptions are self-serving—most philosophical assumptions are.

7. Binnie, I. (2013) *Nevada*. New York, NY: Topside Press, p.6.

Gender and Politics

1. Deleuze, G. and Guattari, F. (1987) *A Thousand Plateaus* (translated by B. Massumi). Minneapolis, MN: University of Minnesota Press, p.32.

2. Some trans people dislike the term "transgenderism" as a way to refer to the phenomenon of being transgender because it comes from a clinical, dehumanizing tradition of cis medical professionals "studying" trans people and defining us in their terms. Personally, I don't have a problem with it as a linguistic shorthand for the clunky phrase "phenomenon of being transgender." Furthermore, on a linguistic level, tacking on "-ism" to words is neutral as far as I am concerned, for example "magnetism" as the phenomenon of being magnetic.

3. Serano, J. (2007) *Whipping Girl: A Transsexual Woman on Sexism and the Scapegoating of Femininity*. Berkeley, CA: Seal Press.

4. The term "vegetative state" is slightly outdated. The modern term for the condition is "unresponsive wakefulness syndrome."

5. Serano, J. (2007) *Whipping Girl: A Transsexual Woman on Sexism and the Scapegoating of Femininity*. Berkeley, CA: Seal Press.

6. Jones, Z. (2016) *Alice Dreger, autogynephilia, and the misrepresentation of trans sexualities (Book review:* Galileo's Middle Finger*)*. Available at https://genderanalysis.net/2016/04/alice-dreger-autogynephilia-and-the-misrepresentation-of-trans-sexualities-book-review-galileos-middle-finger.

7. Dennett, D.C. (1996) *Darwin's Dangerous Idea: Evolution and the Meanings of Life*. New York, NY: Simon and Schuster, p.21.

8. de Beauvoir, S. (1953) *The Second Sex* (translated by H.M Parshley). New York, NY: Alfred A. Knopf, p.330.

9. A 2011 study of 324 Swedish transsexuals by the Karolinska Institute. See www.transadvocate.com/fact-check-study-shows-transition-makes-trans-people-suicidal_n_15483.htm.

10. Mill, J.S. (1998, originally published 1863) *Utilitarianism*. New York, NY: Oxford University Press.

11. Harris, D. (2016) "The sacred androgen: the transgender debate." *The Antioch Review*, 74(1), 64–76.

12. Raymond, J. (1979) *The Transsexual Empire: The Making of the She-Male*. Boston, MA: Beacon Press.

Metaphysics and Epistemology

1. An astute reader will notice that this theory is different from the one I argue for in essay 32, "Gender agnosticism," which is that I am agnostic about how the sex/gender distinction applies to my own case. My final position is closer to this view. However, I still think it is a valuable intellectual exercise to think carefully about the arguments against the sex/gender distinction.

2. Stoller, R.J. (1976, originally published 1968) *Sex and Gender*, vol. 1. New York, NY: Science House, 1976.

3. Morris, J. (1974) *Conundrum*. New York, NY: Harcourt Brace Jovanovich, p.104.

4. Preciado, P. (2013) *Testo Junkie: Sex, Drugs, and Biopolitics in the Pharmacopornographic Era*. New York, NY: The Feminist Press, p.127.

5. Sometimes this goes by "radical feminism" or "trans exclusionary radical feminism" but as many have pointed out, we should not be so quick to relinquish the term "radical" for such deeply conservative views about the relationship between sex and gender.

6. Preciado, P. (2013) *Testo Junkie: Sex, Drugs, and Biopolitics in the Pharmacopornographic Era*. New York, NY: The Feminist Press, p.263.

7. Fausto-Sterling, A. (2000) *Sexing the Body: Gender Politics and the Construction of Sexuality*. New York, NY: Basic Books.

8. https://libcom.org/library/gender-nihilism-anti-manifesto.

Autobiographical Notes

1. I'm using "queer women" as a catch-all for lesbians and bi/pan women. I apologize to those who hate the term "queer"—often language is so inadequate for these purposes but I could think of no other word.

2. There's also a sense in which a couple that is philosophically committed to poly can be "practically" monogamous just in virtue of the circumstances. For example, Jacqueline and I considered ourselves poly and thus open but since we are planning on moving to another city in the near future we haven't felt like developing new relationships with people.

3. Lakoff, G. and Johnson, M. (1999) *Philosophy in the Flesh: The Embodied Mind and its Challenge to Western Thought*. New York, NY: Basic Books.

4. Taleb, N. (2012) *Antifragile*. New York, NY: Random House.

5. I wrote this essay when I was in the throes of a three-month long u-haul relationship. It's now over and I'm living by myself, single, and loving it.

6. "By Trans for Trans" is the motto of St. Louis' Metro Trans Umbrella Group, a local nonprofit organization that runs support groups and events, and works to bring the St. Louis trans community together.

7. See also in this book, essay 23: "Autogynephilia, the gift that keeps on giving."

INDEX